INDIE
PUBLISHING

INDIE

PUBLISHING

HOW TO DESIGN AND PRODUCE YOUR OWN BOOK

Edited by Ellen Lupton

PRINCETON ARCHITECTURAL PRESS, NEW YORK

MARYLAND INSTITUTE COLLEGE OF ART, BALTIMORE

Published by
Princeton Architectural Press
37 East Seventh Street
New York, New York 10003

For a free catalog of books, call 1.800.722.6657

Visit our website at www.papress.com

Library of Congress Cataloging-in-Publication Data
Indie publishing : how to design & produce your own book /
edited by Ellen Lupton.
     p. cm. — (Design briefs)
  Includes bibliographical references and index.
  ISBN 978-1-56898-760-6 (alk. paper)
1. Self-publishing—Handbooks, manuals, etc. 2. Publishers and
publishing—Handbooks, manuals, etc. 3. Book industries and
trade—Handbooks, manuals, etc. 4. Electronic publishing—
Handbooks, manuals, etc. 5. Book design—Handbooks,
manuals, etc. I. Lupton, Ellen. II. Maryland Institute, College
of Art.
     Z285.5.I53 2008
     070.5'93—dc22
                                      2008017325

Special thanks to the staff at Princeton Architectural Press:
Nettie Aljian, Sara Bader, Dorothy Ball, Nicola Bednarek, Janet
Behning, Becca Casbon, Carina Cha, Penny (Yuen Pik) Chu,
Russell Fernandez, Pete Fitzpatrick, Wendy Fuller, Jan Haux,
Aileen Kwun, Nancy Eklund Later, Linda Lee, Aaron Lim, Laurie
Manfra, Katharine Myers, Lauren Nelson Packard, Jennifer
Thompson, Arnoud Verhaeghe, Paul Wagner, Joseph Weston,
and Deb Wood—*Kevin C. Lippert, publisher*

Book Design
Graphic Design MFA Studio,
Maryland Institute College of Art

Editor, Princeton Architectural Press
Clare Jacobson

Art Direction/Style Police
Joseph Galbreath
Lindsey M. Muir

Cover Design
Kelley McIntyre

Inside Covers
Lindsey M. Muir

Divider Pages
Kim Bentley

Research and Design
Kim Bentley
Kristian Bjørnard
Jeremy Botts
Ryan Clifford
Viviana Cordova
John Corrigan
Danielle Davis
Joseph Galbreath
Joo Ha
HyunSoo Lim
Ellen Lupton
Gregory May
Kelley McIntyre
Lindsey M. Muir
Jason Okutake
April Osmanof
Jennifer Cole Phillips
Yue Tuo
Tony Venne

Typefaces
Auto and Dolly, designed by Underware
Vinyl, designed by John P. Corrigan

This project was initiated by
The Center for Design Thinking
Maryland Institute College of Art.

CONTENTS

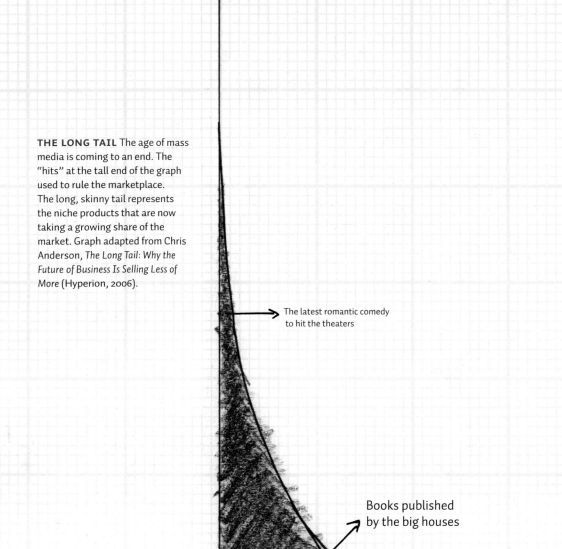

The Harry Potter series

THE LONG TAIL The age of mass media is coming to an end. The "hits" at the tall end of the graph used to rule the marketplace. The long, skinny tail represents the niche products that are now taking a growing share of the market. Graph adapted from Chris Anderson, *The Long Tail: Why the Future of Business Is Selling Less of More* (Hyperion, 2006).

The latest romantic comedy to hit the theaters

Books published by the big houses

Illustration by Kelley McIntyre

About this Book

THIS HANDBOOK PRESENTS BASIC INFORMATION ABOUT PUBLISHING YOUR OWN BOOK, WHETHER INFORMALLY FOR FRIENDS OR FAMILY OR IN A MORE OFFICIAL WAY. Perhaps you want to commemorate your grandfather's life with selections from his war diaries. Maybe you need a full-color catalog for your first gallery exhibition. Maybe a wonderful old building in your neighborhood is about to be torn down, and a short history of the site could help save it. If you work with kids after school, a book of their poetry could show the community what they've achieved. If you have content that you want to share and you want to give it a fresh and orderly form, this book will help you get started.

The cult B movie you rented from Netflix

Your old roommate's literary zine

This book

The rise of self-publishing activities in recent years is part of what writer Chris Anderson has called "the long tail." According to Anderson, the age of mass media is coming to an end. We now live in a world that supports an enormous range of content tailored to a literally endless diversity of people. The tall but narrow peak at the beginning of Anderson's graph represents the best-sellers—the "hits" that used to rule the marketplace. The long, skinny part represents the niche products that sell far fewer copies individually than any one hit, but as a group are commanding a larger and larger share of the market. The "long tail" is populated by blogs, independent music and video, zines, short-run books and novels, machinima, and countless other small-scale, niche-oriented endeavors.

The long tail is fed by the democratization of production tools (such as blogging software, digicams, and Photoshop) and the rise of web-based forms of distribution (such as Netflix, Amazon, eBay, Etsy, YouTube, and Google). The long tail—and demand for its products—is virtually infinite. As the tail winds down to the 100,000th-most-downloaded song, to the 400,000th-, to the 500,000th-, there are still songs out there that are being downloaded somewhere by someone. The vitality of the long tail proves that human beings really do have an appetite for something more exotic than James Bond and Danielle Steel.

The publishing world is being transformed by new social attitudes about making and sharing content. More and more people see themselves not just as consumers of media but also as producers. Anyone who gets seriously caught up in a subject—from collecting stamps to sewing stuffed animals—ends up building a body of knowledge, gained from direct experience as well as from classes, clubs, books, and online sources. The passionate amateur often wants to share that knowledge with others, contributing to a collective information base. Making books is one way to do that, and it is getting easier and easier to do it on your own.

The short film you
saw on YouTube

Your book?

Indie Publishing introduces readers, writers, and makers to the process of producing their own books, with an emphasis on design. This book is about putting together content in compelling and practical formats. Book design involves planning how content will be structured (a flow and sequence of materials) and how it will be assembled into printed pages (a physical object that can be held in your hands).

The *Indie Publishing* project was initiated by the Center for Design Thinking at Maryland Institute College of Art. The center works with students and faculty to author, produce, and disseminate design research directed at a variety of audiences.

Our book offers general information about design and production that is relevant to any publishing project as well as case studies of particular types of book that you might want to make and share, from a collection of poems to a children's book or exhibition catalog. Throughout this volume, you will see inspiring examples of beautiful and original books created by independent authors, artists, and designers. If you are a creative person with content you want to share, then dive in and get going.

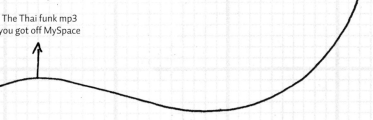

The Thai funk mp3
you got off MySpace

ONE OF A KIND

A handmade scrapbook is an object to cherish for years to come. Jennifer Williams is a college professor and DIY designer who made this handcrafted book in honor of her daughter Alice. She used an antique album as a base.

PUBLISHING BASICS

by Ellen Lupton and Kelley McIntyre

A PUBLISHED WORK APPEARS IN MORE THAN ONE COPY AND IS AVAILABLE, IN SOME FASHION, TO AN AUDIENCE, LARGE OR SMALL. Publishing can be local and handmade, or it can address vast audiences around the world. Making a one-of-a-kind scrapbook isn't really publishing, but producing multiple copies of a book of photographs and giving it to friends and family members is an informal kind of distribution.

For a work to be published in a more official way, it needs to be accessible to a broader audience, becoming part of a shared discourse—the public record. A published work is put out into the world where anyone might see it. Publishing involves bravery and risk: it is entrepreneurial in an intellectual as well as a financial sense. To publish is to put yourself out there and proclaim that you have content worth sharing.

SOME OF A KIND
Graphic designer Laurie DeMartino made this beautiful hardcover book to celebrate the birth of her baby daughter, Grace. She had the book offset printed and sent it to friends and family.

Publishing involves both producing and distributing a work. First you have to present your content in a physical form that people can understand, and then you have to make it possible for people to find it. (If you have 5,000 printed copies of a book sitting in your basement, that book isn't really available to the public; it has been produced, but not distributed.) It used to be that books and magazines could only be found in libraries and bookstores, and it was difficult to get independently produced publications into those places. Today, there are more ways for small content-makers to reach an audience.

The publisher of a book is like the producer of a movie, responsible for deciding that a particular work is worthy of being edited, designed, printed, bound, marketed, and distributed. The publisher puts up the money and finds the people or services who will make all those things happen; the ultimate goal is to get the book into the hands of readers by selling it to booksellers and distributors or directly to the public.

The publishing industry in the United States used to be a narrow community, located mostly in New York City and controlled by a small, elite group. Today, although a few international corporations dominate the mainstream publishing business, smaller-scale ventures are starting up everywhere, thanks to new technologies and new ways to make, buy, and sell books. More and more publishers are creating works directed at niche audiences (from Beatlemaniacs to snow globe collectors), and they are using the internet to reach readers directly.

Independent publishing covers a range of ventures, from the initiation of a single book project by a lone author to ongoing endeavors launched by organizations or individuals. Thousands of small publishing houses around the world produce books in relatively small quantities and distribute them online as well as through bookstores.

Some self-publishing services (such as Lulu.com) work with an author's print-ready digital files, while others provide editing, design, printing, marketing, and distribution services for a fee. In contrast, commercial trade publishers take on the cost of all such services and (usually) pay the author for creating content. Pay-to-publish establishments often are dismissed with the term "vanity press," but those negative connotations are changing as small-scale, self-initiated ventures become more vital and widespread. In music, film, art, and journalism, the idea of "independent" media is now accepted and even celebrated by artists who also want to be entrepreneurs and who want to work outside the mainstream industry.

By becoming a publisher, the author gains a lot of freedom. He or she also takes on financial risk as well as responsibility for all the details of making a book and putting it out into the world. Why would anyone assume this arduous set of tasks when an entire profession and business system (the publishing industry) is already in place to perform it? Many people

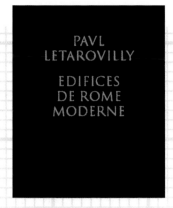

PAVL
LETAROVILLY

EDIFICES
DE ROME
MODERNE

PROFILE: KEVIN LIPPERT
founded Princeton Architectural
Press in 1981 when he was a graduate
student at the Princeton University
School of Architecture. Why did
Lippert publish his first book? Because
he wanted his own copy of Paul
Letarouilly's *Edifices de Rome Moderne*,
an eighteenth-century design classic.
Laziness, he recalls, drove him into
publishing: "I wanted a copy of my
own so that I wouldn't have to deal
with the elephant volume on reserve
in the library." Lippert produced the
book with a $5,000 student loan. Since
"Princeton" is the name of a town
as well as a university, he used the
name to bring gravitas to his fledgling
enterprise. After finishing school, he
took on more and more publishing
projects. His press grew to become
an internationally known publisher
of books on architecture and design.
Princeton Architectural Press books
(including the one you are reading) are
now distributed throughout North and
South America by Chronicle Books.

start their own publishing ventures because
they don't have access to the official
publishing establishment—they don't know
the right people, they don't yet have
reputations as authors, they've been turned
down by editors and agents, they are working
in a new or unusual genre, or they are writing
for specialized or underserved markets. Others
want complete control over the design and
presentation of their books. Some authors or
institutions do their own publishing in order
to get their work out more quickly, while
others enjoy the entrepreneurial thrill of
making a product and seeing it through its life
cycle. By shouldering the risk, they stand to
reap the profits if their venture succeeds.

Indeed, most successful publishing
houses begin as the vision of an enterprising
individual (or group). These small businesses
sometimes grow into profitable—or at least
self-sustaining—entities. Most publishing
ventures, however, are motivated not so much
by profit as by the desire to share ideas. This
handbook speaks to authors and artists who
are just beginning to experiment with the idea
of independent publishing.

Be warned: publishing a book, like
starting a band or building a blog, is an
unlikely way to get rich quick or get famous
fast. Publishing is a painstaking, labor-
intensive craft. Do it because you care about
what you have to say, because you have people
you want to say it to, and because you take
pleasure in making things happen.

Nuts and Bolts

The formal publishing process involves sharing information in an official way that allows booksellers, libraries, publishers, and search engines to know that your work exists. How crucial are these technicalities to your project? It depends on how you plan to distribute your book.

ISBNs and ISSNs

An ISBN is a thirteen-digit International Standard Book Number; an ISSN is an eight-digit International Standard Serial Number (for magazines). These numbers constitute a unique address for your publication, identifying its publisher as well as its title and geographic origin. No two ISBNs or ISSNs are the same.

Do you need an ISBN? If you want to distribute your book via bookstores, libraries, Amazon, museum shops, and other commercial channels, then you will need one. If you are using your book only as a gift, a promotional item, a personal portfolio, a memento, or for any purpose other than retail, then an ISBN is not necessary.

You will need a new ISBN any time you substantially revise the content or design of your book. Every version of your book requires a separate ISBN, including paperback, hardcover, audio versions, and so on. ISBNs are sold to publishers in blocks of 10, 100, 1,000, and 10,000. In order to purchase them, you must register as a publisher through the ISBN agency of your geographic area. For publishers with an address in the United States, U.S. Virgin Islands, Guam, and Puerto Rico, the United States ISBN Agency is authorized to assign them. You can apply for ISBNs directly through the agency, or you can acquire them (and thus become registered as a publisher) through various print-on-demand services.

Barcodes

The barcode for a publication represents its ISBN or ISSN as well as pricing information in a font that can be read by scanning equipment. Having a barcode is essential if you want to distribute your book in stores. Barcodes are available from various publishing services, which are easily found online. You need to have your ISBN or ISSN before getting a barcode. Many print-on-demand companies can provide you with one as part of their services.

Anatomy of a Barcode

1. The ISBN

This digit represents **the country of origin**: 0 and 1 are used for English-speaking countries.

The center group of numbers represents **the publisher**.

These digits identify **the title**. It can be two to five digits long, depending on the size of the publisher number.

Last is **the check digit**, a mathematical variable of the first twelve, which validates the ISBN.

The first three digits identify the type of **product**. "978" is a book. "979" will start being used when more ISBNs are needed.

This number indicates the price. The "5" means that the price is in U.S. dollars. The next four digits represent the price in pennies (this book is $21.95).

978-1-56898-760-6

52195

9 781568 987606

4. The Code

"978" is the **Bookland EAN**, a "country" code reserved for books and related products.

The EAN matches the ISBN-13.

2. The EAN-5

3. The EAN

---

1. THE ISBN
The ISBN appears at the top as well as the bottom of the barcode to make it easier for cashiers to find when their barcode scanners aren't working and they have to type in the ISBN by hand.

2. THE EAN-5
This smaller bar code is a five-digit add-on that encodes the retail price of the publication. The first digit represents the currency, while the remaining digits indicate the price. U.S. dollars are represented by the number five. An EAN-5 of 52195 translates to $21.95.

3. THE EAN
The EAN, or European Article Number, provides world-wide standardization in the sale and handling of all retail products.

4. THE CODE
The barcode is basically the EAN in binary; the shorter lines represent the numbers, while the three longer "guard bars" indicate where the different sections of the number begin and end.

Anatomy of a Copyright Page

The publisher's name and address,

Published by
Princeton Architectural Press
37 East Seventh Street
New York, New York 10003

The copyright line, for text, illustrations, or cited excerpts

© 2008 Princeton Architectural Press
All rights reserved
Printed and bound in China

The country of origin is required for importing.

This number indicates the publishing history. The number to the far right in each group is the telling number. This book was printed in 2008, and this is the first printing. When each additional printing is run, numbers are removed from the right accordingly.

11 10 09 08   4 3 2 1
First Edition

No part of this book may be used or reproduced in any manner without written permission from the publisher, except in the context of reviews.

Every reasonable attempt has been made to identify owners of copyright. Errors or omissions will be corrected in subsequent editions.

Cover your tail.

The final page count goes here, but since the CIP data is aquired long before the design is final, spaces are left for them to be written in later.

Library of Congress Cataloging-in-Publication Data
Indie publishing : how to design & produce your own book / edited by Ellen Lupton.
    p. cm. — (Design briefs)
  Includes bibliographical references and index.
  ISBN 978-1-56898-760-6 (alk. paper)
1. Self-publishing—Handbooks, manuals, etc. 2. Publishers and publishing—Handbooks, manuals, etc. 3. Book industries and trade—Handbooks, manuals, etc. 4. Electronic publishing—Handbooks, manuals, etc. 5. Book design—Handbooks, manuals, etc. I. Lupton, Ellen. II. Maryland Institute, College of Art.
    Z285.5.I53 2008
    070.5'93—dc22

This book was printed on acid-free paper.

Subjects and codes used for cataloging

2008017325

Credits are optional, but they add interest to an otherwise dull page, and they provide an opportunity to acknowledge the people, places, and materials that made your book possible. It's amazing how many people contribute to the creation of a book.

Special thanks to the staff at Princeton Architectural Press:
Nettie Aljian, Sara Bader, Dorothy Ball, Nicola Bednarek, Janet Behning, Becca Casbon, Carina Cha, Penny (Yuen Pik) Chu, Russell Fernandez, Pete Fitzpatrick, Wendy Fuller, Jan Haux, Aileen Kwun, Nancy Eklund Later, Linda Lee, Aaron Lim, Laurie Manfra, Katharine Myers, Lauren Nelson Packard, Jennifer Thompson, Arnoud Verhaeghe, Paul Wagner, Joseph Weston, and Deb Wood — *Kevin C. Lippert, publisher*

Copyrights

Copyright laws were developed in the eighteenth century to protect authors' and publishers' economic interest in their work for a period of time. When you embark on your own publishing project, it's important to understand how you want to protect your work, as well as how to avoid violating the copyrights of other creators.

In the United States, every creative work is automatically protected by copyright the moment it is produced. Thus, any image or text that you find out in the world or on the internet is subject to copyright protection, with the exception of works published over seventy years ago whose copyrights have not been explicitly renewed.

Some ways of implementing copyrighted material are considered "fair use." For example, it is acceptable to quote a short passage from an essay or book for purposes of commentary and interpretation. Certain forms of parody are considered fair use, as long as they don't become a new work or product that directly competes with the content being parodied. For example, you might get away with printing a parodic send-up of *Martha Stewart Living*, but it would be asking for trouble to create an original lifestyle magazine using the goddess's name or image. Various pictures and documents are in the "public domain," meaning that they can be quoted, sampled, and republished by anyone. You can access many of these through the United States Library of Congress, www.loc.gov.

By making it illegal for one publisher to copy the work of another without payment or permission, copyright law aims to stimulate creativity. Why would you bother to become an artist or author if everyone could use your material (and profit from it) without paying or acknowledging you? Copyrights can also restrict creativity, however, by making it difficult to reissue, reinterpret, or comment on existing works. For example, it is illegal to include the "Happy Birthday" song in a film or play without paying a fee to the publisher that owns the copyright to the song.

Many creative producers actually *want* other artists to interpret and disseminate their work, thus giving their ideas a new life for new audiences. Creative Commons provides tools for producing custom copyright licenses, replacing the standard notice "All Rights Reserved" with the refreshingly open "Some Rights Reserved." For example, you could allow noncommercial uses of your work while requiring that any republisher attribute your name to your work when they use it.

CIP and Copyright Services

THE COPYRIGHT CLEARANCE CENTER was established to make it easier for authors and publishers to sell and acquire rights to published texts. www.copyright.com

CREATIVE COMMONS is an activist organization that is trying to change the nature of intellectual property. Go there to build your own customized copyright license. www.creativecommons.org

PROFILE: EDWARD TUFTE is the author and publisher of an influential series of books about information design. When Tufte set out to produce *The Visual Display of Quantitative Information*, publishers told him that they couldn't provide the quality of printing, paper, and color reproduction that he demanded because it would make the retail cost of his book too high. So Tufte decided to publish the book himself. He created his own company, Graphics Press, and took out a mortgage on his house to finance it. By publishing the book himself, he was able to keep the price accessible and maintain control over every aspect of the book's design and production. "Making the book," he says, "is part of the scholarship." Shown above, cover of Edward Tufte's *Beautiful Evidence*, published by Graphics Press in 2006.

Books in Print

Books in Print is a database maintained by Bowker (who is also the exclusive U.S. ISBN agency) that lists all the books officially in print in the United States. Bowker publishes a number of international directories as well. Books in Print is used by booksellers and libraries to order books from publishers. It lists the title, author, publisher, price, and ISBN of every book available and its various formats or editions.

CIP Data

Publishers in the United States are encouraged to include in their books information that is generated by the Library of Congress Cataloging in Publication Program. This standard block of information (called CIP data) appears on the copyright page of the book. CIP data lists the author, date, and subject matter of your book, allowing librarians and online booksellers such as Amazon to easily and accurately add your publication to their collections by accessing an electronic database once your book is released. Complete information about acquiring CIP data is available from the Library of Congress at http://cip.loc.gov.

Buying Barcodes and ISBNs

BOWKER/U.S. ISBN AGENCY is the official source for all ISBNs. www.isbn.org

LULU, BOOKSURGE, and other print on demand (POD) services can help you acquire an ISBN and barcode. There is an additional charge for this service.

ONLINE BROKERS can sell you an ISBN, but be wary of these deals, as you want to be sure that your number legitimately establishes you as the publisher of your book.

PUBLISHED BY
Ellen Lupton / Slush Editions
www.elupton.com | www.SexyLibrarianNovel.com

ISBN 978-0-6151-7677-2

```
Weist, Julia.
      Sexy librarian : a novel, critical edition /
Julia Weist ; essay by Jennifer Tobias ; afterword
by Ellen Lupton. -- Baltimore : Slush Editions,
2008.
      172 p. ; 22 cm.
      ISBN 978-0-6151-7677-2
      1. Librarians -- Fiction.  2. Job
satisfaction -- Fiction.  3. Art -- New York
(State) -- New York -- Fiction.  4. Middle West -
- Fiction.  5. Artists' books. I. Tobias, Jennifer.
II. Lupton, Ellen.
      PS3623.I395 S49 2008
      N6535.N5
      Z720.W463
```

ORIGINAL CATALOGING BY
Sherman Clarke, Head of Original Cataloging
New York University Libraries

DIARY OF A CATALOG RECORD

Sexy Librarian is an independently published novel, and it was the first book produced by its publisher, Slush Editions. (The making of *Sexy Librarian* is discussed in detail in the "Fiction" chapter of this book.) The novel is about librarians and libraries, so it was especially important to the author and publisher to include an official catalog record in the book. The Library of Congress won't provide a record for first-time publishers, so the authors asked a prominent librarian, Sherman Clarke, to create a custom catalog record for *Sexy Librarian*. As libraries and booksellers acquire the book, they will use this data.

Sales and Distribution

How do you get your book into people's hands? Bookstores are the classic way, and in the pages that follow, we'll talk about how books end up on the tables and shelves of retailers. Books are sold in many other ways as well—on websites like Amazon, on your own blog, or at special events such as concerts, parties, and gallery openings.

Going Retail

Most books and publications arrive at bookstores via distributors, the biggest one being Ingram Book Group. Such companies allow booksellers to purchase many different titles from one centralized source. By working with a distributor, the publisher's sales staff avoids having to personally travel from store to store selling books. Using a distributor costs money, of course, and thus adds to the retail price of any book.

The suggested retail price of a conventionally published book is typically eight times the cost of printing and shipping each copy (known as the unit cost). This allows for the markup that occurs as the book passes through the various stages of the sales and distribution process: from printer to warehouse to bookstore. Each middleman needs to raise the price to make a profit. (The suggested price is often discounted by big retailers such as Barnes & Noble and Amazon, a practice that gives shoppers even less incentive to patronize independent bookstores.)

The final price of a book should relate not only to the publisher's unit cost (and desired profits) but to what readers might expect to pay. Balance your desire to make a profit against your desire to have people read your book. Print-on-demand books can rarely be sold at an eightfold markup because the unit cost is too high. Look at books similar to yours to help set a viable price. Some indie publishers sell their books directly to their readers via websites, events, fairs, and so on, helping them to keep their prices reasonable while still making a profit on titles sold.

Distribution Services

INGRAM is the big mama of commercial book distributors, but the company has various services tailored to the needs of independent publishers.

SMALL PRESS DISTRIBUTION is a nonprofit organization that distributes works published by over five hundred independent presses.

INDEPENDENT PUBLISHERS GROUP works exclusively with small presses and independent publishers.

D.A.P./DISTRIBUTED ART PUBLISHERS specializes in distributing art books created by museums, galleries, and small presses. If D.A.P. likes your book, they can help get it into museum stores and specialty bookstores.

BIBLIOTOPIA

This book is published by David R. Godine, a long-standing independent publisher in Boston. We purchased it at Joseph Fox Bookshop, a family-owned store in Philadelphia that carries numerous independent-press titles. Design and illustration by Elliott Banfield. Reproduced by permission of David R. Godine, Publisher, Inc. Copyright © 2005 by Elliott Banfield. Photograph by Jason Okutake.

Anatomy of a Bookstore

BY KELLEY MCINTYRE

Bookstores, *tiny*? Not where I live. Here, the small neighborhood nook is slowly giving way to massive megastores with more choices, and coffee drinks, than many of us had even ten years ago. Intrepid gal that I am, I took it upon myself to tackle one of these monsters and see what makes it tick. Five days, eighteen hours, ten cups of coffee, and one nosy clerk later, I feel I can call myself a bookstore expert. Here, in explicit detail, I share my wealth of knowledge and experience with you. Use it well.

LEGEND

- = fiction
- = nonfiction
- = kids and teens
- = reference
- = bargain books
- = stationery
- = backrooms and restrooms
- = new releases
- = favorite and seasonal titles
- = highlighted series
- = novelty items
- **?** = information
- **$** = registers
- **C** = cafe

COMMON QUESTIONS:

Where did all the chairs go?!
When new stores open, the designers fill them up with big, cushy armchairs to encourage you to linger. But a few weeks or months later, once you're hooked on the place, they slowly remove the chairs until about half as many remain. Most people barely notice.

How do I get my book on one of those fancy displays?
Some of the books sitting out on tables are selected by the bookstore's managers or staff. In other instances, publishers pay a fee to have their titles featured on display tables, endcaps, and ladders——devices that help books float to the top of a sea of choices. The big chains can influence what books are published and even how they are designed, owing to the volume of their sales.

What's in that room behind the toilets?
Theories run wild on this one, but here's what I think: a strange land of fidgety fawns, cockney beavers, and never-ending winter; a twenty-four-hour disco; or staff offices, stockrooms, and a loading dock.

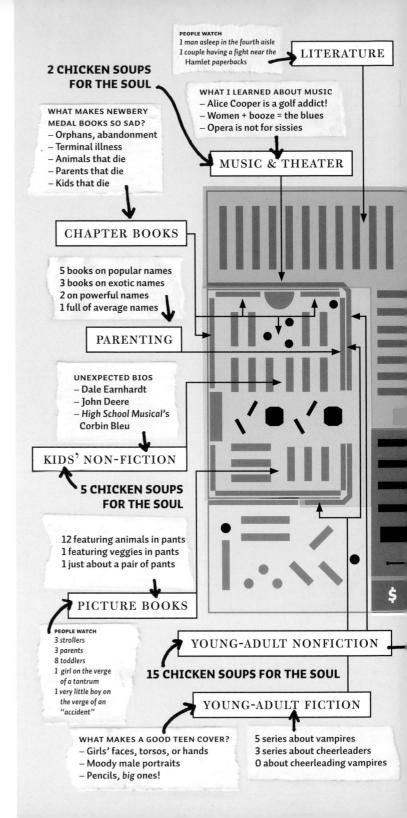

PEOPLE WATCH
1 *man asleep in the fourth aisle*
1 *couple having a fight near the Hamlet paperbacks*

LITERATURE

2 CHICKEN SOUPS FOR THE SOUL

WHAT I LEARNED ABOUT MUSIC
– Alice Cooper is a golf addict!
– Women + booze = the blues
– Opera is not for sissies

WHAT MAKES NEWBERY MEDAL BOOKS SO SAD?
– Orphans, abandonment
– Terminal illness
– Animals that die
– Parents that die
– Kids that die

MUSIC & THEATER

CHAPTER BOOKS

5 books on popular names
3 books on exotic names
2 on powerful names
1 full of average names

PARENTING

UNEXPECTED BIOS
– Dale Earnhardt
– John Deere
– *High School Musical*'s Corbin Bleu

KIDS' NON-FICTION

5 CHICKEN SOUPS FOR THE SOUL

12 featuring animals in pants
1 featuring veggies in pants
1 just about a pair of pants

PICTURE BOOKS

PEOPLE WATCH
3 *strollers*
3 *parents*
8 *toddlers*
1 *girl on the verge of a tantrum*
1 *very little boy on the verge of an "accident"*

YOUNG-ADULT NONFICTION

15 CHICKEN SOUPS FOR THE SOUL

YOUNG-ADULT FICTION

WHAT MAKES A GOOD TEEN COVER?
– Girls' faces, torsos, or hands
– Moody male portraits
– Pencils, *big* ones!

5 series about vampires
3 series about cheerleaders
0 about cheerleading vampires

$

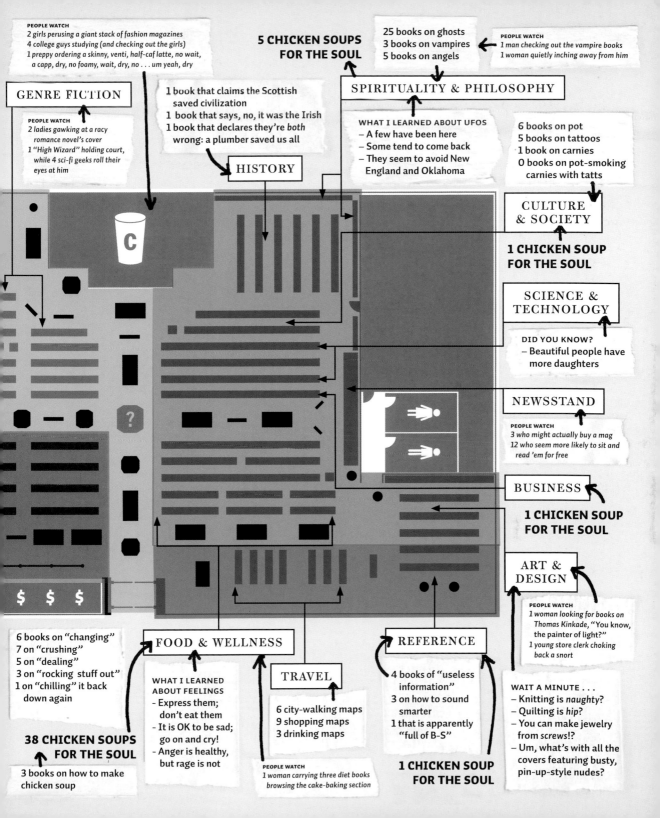

PEOPLE WATCH
2 girls perusing a giant stack of fashion magazines
4 college guys studying (and checking out the girls)
1 preppy ordering a skinny, venti, half-caf latte, no wait, a capp, dry, no foamy, wait, dry, no . . . um yeah, dry

5 CHICKEN SOUPS FOR THE SOUL

25 books on ghosts
3 books on vampires
5 books on angels

PEOPLE WATCH
1 man checking out the vampire books
1 woman quietly inching away from him

GENRE FICTION

PEOPLE WATCH
2 ladies gawking at a racy romance novel's cover
1 "High Wizard" holding court, while 4 sci-fi geeks roll their eyes at him

1 book that claims the Scottish saved civilization
1 book that says, no, it was the Irish
1 book that declares they're *both* wrong: a plumber saved us all

SPIRITUALITY & PHILOSOPHY

WHAT I LEARNED ABOUT UFOS
– A few have been here
– Some tend to come back
– They seem to avoid New England and Oklahoma

6 books on pot
5 books on tattoos
1 book on carnies
0 books on pot-smoking carnies with tatts

HISTORY

CULTURE & SOCIETY

1 CHICKEN SOUP FOR THE SOUL

SCIENCE & TECHNOLOGY

DID YOU KNOW?
– Beautiful people have more daughters

NEWSSTAND

PEOPLE WATCH
3 who might actually buy a mag
12 who seem more likely to sit and read 'em for free

BUSINESS

1 CHICKEN SOUP FOR THE SOUL

ART & DESIGN

PEOPLE WATCH
1 woman looking for books on Thomas Kinkade, "You know, the painter of light?"
1 young store clerk choking back a snort

6 books on "changing"
7 on "crushing"
5 on "dealing"
3 on "rocking stuff out"
1 on "chilling" it back down again

FOOD & WELLNESS

WHAT I LEARNED ABOUT FEELINGS
– Express them; don't eat them
– It is OK to be sad; go on and cry!
– Anger is healthy, but rage is not

TRAVEL

6 city-walking maps
9 shopping maps
3 drinking maps

REFERENCE

4 books of "useless information"
3 on how to sound smarter
1 that is apparently "full of B-S"

WAIT A MINUTE . . .
– Knitting is *naughty*?
– Quilting is *hip*?
– You can make jewelry from *screws*!?
– Um, what's with all the covers featuring busty, pin-up-style nudes?

38 CHICKEN SOUPS FOR THE SOUL

3 books on how to make chicken soup

PEOPLE WATCH
1 woman carrying three diet books browsing the cake-baking section

1 CHICKEN SOUP FOR THE SOUL

PROFILE: CARY TENNIS writes a popular advice column on Salon.com. When Tennis pitched an anthology of his favorite pieces to commercial publishers, "The project just got weird and twisted and died." Since he has an avid fan base (what's called a "platform" in the publishing biz), he decided to produce the book himself and sell it online directly to his readers.

Since You Asked features long, unfettered letters from readers about dark personal problems, followed by even longer responses from Tennis. Yet publishers had wanted pithy sound bites instead. Tennis explains that the editors he contacted "did not understand the culture we were operating in, this freewheeling, intensely vocal, intellectual, contemplative, argumentative internet culture centered around Salon and its iconoclastic writers and politics." Furthermore, Tennis had learned from disgruntled author friends that while publishers front the money to print a title, they often do little to promote or sustain it. And yet they seek control of its look, feel, and voice.

Control is exactly what Tennis wanted, so he decided to publish the book himself. Luckily for him, his wife, Norma Tennis, is a professional graphic designer. "I wanted control over content and design," say Tennis. "And I knew I could not handle having all that intimate stuff, of passionate interest to me and my wife, turned over to someone who did not know us and our attitudes." An initial print run of 3,000 books arrived in 107 cartons containing 28 books each, stacked in their garage and basement. Sending the books out one by one makes Cary and Norma feel personally connected with their readers.

Selling Online

If you or your organization has a website, it's easy to set up your own online "store" using services such as PayPal. You can sell your book directly to customers and avoid the hassle and expense of finding a distributor. Even a MySpace or Facebook page can be a sales tool for your titles. You don't need an ISBN to sell your book on your own website; you simply need to present it to potential buyers in a compelling way—and be sure to mail it promptly!

Any book with an ISBN can be included in Amazon's enormous database of products. If you are distributing the book yourself, you can sell it via Amazon by setting up a Marketplace merchant account; Amazon collects a percentage of each sale, but asks for no payment up front. If your book is distributed by a POD service or an independent press association, your distributor will most likely fulfill the orders that come through Amazon.

But how will potential readers know about your book? Authors and publishers can promote their books online by becoming Amazon Associates. This free service allows you to lead customers from your own blog or website directly to Amazon's selling machine. The author receives a referral fee from Amazon for every book sold through the author's link.

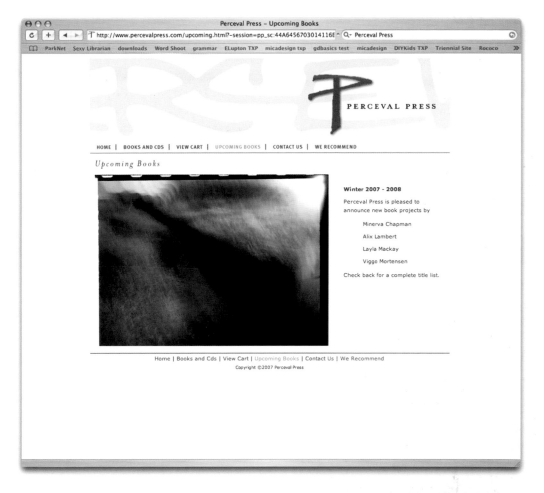

PROFILE: VIGGO MORTENSEN is the actor who played Aragorn in *Lord of the Rings* and the likable psychopath in David Cronenberg's *A History of Violence*. He also is the founder of Perceval Press, an independent publishing house that produces a dozen or so titles a year. The press publishes books on art, photography, philosophy, and politics. Shown here is the web page and the cover for a book of photographs by Viggo Mortensen. Books from Perceval Press are sold primarily online at Percevalpress.com.

Marketing

Even if your book is published through commercial publishing channels, you, the author, are your project's most important promoter. Build your own book tour by offering to speak at schools, libraries, bookstores, museums, galleries, and anywhere else you might connect with potential readers. (Dream on about your prepaid cross-country promotional junket, chatting up your latest title with the local literati at Starbucks or Barnes & Noble. Book tours like that are the privilege of only the most established authors.) Success breeds success. Use your appearances and press clips to entice booksellers to carry your book or to drum up more readings or speaking engagements.

YOUR WEBSITE OR BLOG is a great place to talk about your book (and offer it for sale, either directly or through Amazon or another online seller). Make it easy for journalists and bloggers to write about you by providing images, excerpts, author photos, and other information.

REVIEW COPIES are free books that you send to journalists who might write about your project. This gets pricey, so consider sending review copies only on request, as a follow-up to your press release or other publicity materials.

BOOK PARTIES build buzz around your project. Who to invite? Your friends, the press, and everyone involved with the project. Be creative: hold the party at an interesting bar or restaurant, or invite a band to add excitement.

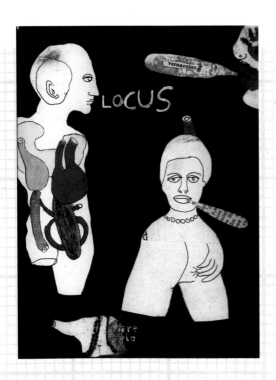

PROFILE: LOCUS is an independently produced magazine published in Baltimore that features work primarily by Baltimore-area artists and writers. *Locus* is edited, designed, and published by Emily J. Hunter and Arthur Soontornsaratool. Produced on a digital press, the print run is under 500. To launch each issue, the publishers have a big party where they sell copies for ten dollars each. *Locus* is a local magazine, and most copies sell out at the launch party, so the distribution problem is solved right there. Cover art by Luca Dipierro.

How to Write a Press Release

INDIE PUBLISHING
HOW TO DESIGN AND PRODUCE YOUR OWN BOOK

October 20, 2008
Contact: Ellen Lupton
www.papress.com

New Book Shows Designers, Authors, and Artists How to Put Their Work into Print

Print isn't dead; it's just getting started. The digital revolution has made it easier for independent authors to put their work into print and distribute it to audiences far and wide. This handy manual, published by Princeton Architectural Press, demystifies the process of designing, producing, and distributing printed matter at a variety of scales, from handmade editions to print-on-demand and mass production.

Indie Publishing invites readers to explore the creative design process through a series of visual case studies of compelling book genres, including fiction, poetry, zines, exhibition catalogs, children's books, and artists' portfolios. Design principles such as scale, cropping, pacing, and typography are explored, along with commentary on how to create effective and intriguing title pages, tables of contents, captions, and more. It also takes readers through the process of creating marketing materials for a publishing project. If you've always wanted to get your words in print, this book will show you how to do it yourself.

A how-to-make-it section takes readers step by step through the production of books, using handmade and digital means. Learn how to bind a book, set type, create layouts, and prepare a book for production.

Indie Publishing is designed and authored by students and faculty in the Graphic Design MFA program at Maryland Institute College of Art (MICA). It is illustrated with groundbreaking work by independent designers and publishers.

Layout the release on letterhead, featuring the book's logo. Your book doesn't have a logo? Make one based on your cover graphics.

Don't be shy. Open your letter with a tag line that will catch attention.

Don't forget to include the date as well as your contact information.

The vital facts should appear in your first paragraph; this text will be used directly by journalists to create event listings for a local paper.

Use an interesting paper stock to add a jolt of personality to your release—just be careful that the design doesn't fight the tone or content of your message.

DESIGN YOUR OWN BOOKS

Design Basics—Fiction—Poetry—Zines—Picture Books for Kids—Picture Books for Adults

Exhibition Catalogs—Portfolios

alphonso

My father shot this in 1976, two years before I was born. Since I started carrying it (I call him Rudy) from place to place, no apartment feels like mine until I hang him up. The place could be a total wreck, with boxes everywhere and no place to sit or sleep or walk, but as soon as I get him on the wall, it's home. He usually acknowledges the main entrance. I like to see him either as I enter or as I leave the apartment. Alphonso was added when I decorated Rudy for Halloween one year.

DEER HEAD (RUDY) :: ABOVE THE DOOR :: 6 YEARS :: DAD SHOT IT

DECISIONS, DECISIONS This limited-edition book creates a portrait of a person through special objects from his home. Each spread presents an artifact and keys it to its placement in different apartments over time. The designer made numerous decisions before arriving at the book's final form, including page size (6.5 x 8 inches), typeface (Granjon), printing (inkjet), paper (Stonehenge cream), and binding (hand-sewn signatures). Designed by Kim Bentley.

DESIGN BASICS

by Joseph Galbreath

WHEN YOU PICK UP A BOOK AND READ IT, YOU MAY RARELY STOP TO THINK ABOUT WHO DESIGNED IT. Yet every book has been put together by creative people who have paid attention to every aspect of its making, from the size of the pages to the design of the cover to the choice of the binding and paper. Although the front of a commercial book typically uses bold type and imagery to call attention to itself, the interior pages are often subtle and discreet, making way for the process of reading.

Book design is an art. Anyone who tries to design even a simple book will quickly discover how difficult this art can be. If you are new to graphic design, keep your initial endeavors as simple as possible and look closely at other books for inspiration. There is a long tradition of book making, and by modeling your book on what has gone before, you are more likely to create a volume that feels classic, professional, and appealing to readers.

The book design process is closely intertwined with production and manufacturing—how your book is physically constructed. This chapter looks at basic principles of sequence, page design, typography, and cover design. As you begin the design process, you will also need to keep in mind how your book will be made. Refer to our section titled "Make Your Own Books" for ideas. You may decide that working with a professional designer is the best route for your project, but as an independent publisher, you will want to familiarize yourself with the process.

Anatomy of a Book

Nearly every book has a beginning, a middle, and an end. Shown here is an overview of how a published volume is typically organized.

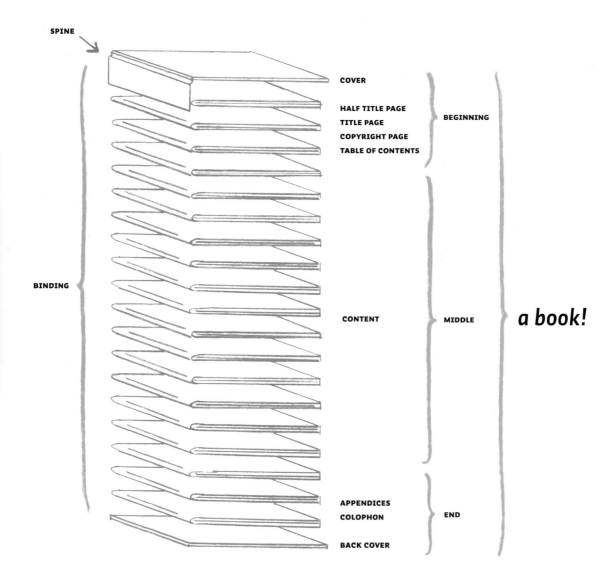

SPINE

COVER

HALF TITLE PAGE
TITLE PAGE
COPYRIGHT PAGE
TABLE OF CONTENTS

BEGINNING

BINDING

CONTENT

MIDDLE

a book!

APPENDICES
COLOPHON

END

BACK COVER

Text Book

A novel and some works of nonfiction consist primarily of text, although they might feature occasional illustrations, such as a frontispiece at the opening of the book, small drawings at the start of each chapter, or diagrams keyed to the text.

Most text books have one main column of type, called the body. The margins can be even all around, or you can create wider margins at the center (to keep content away from the binding), or along the outside edge (to create room for the reader's hands). Some designers like a wide margin along the bottom, providing a place for the reader's hands.

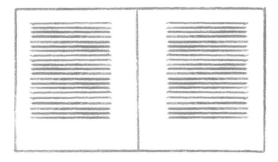

BASIC TEXT BOOK

Picture Book

In photo albums, exhibition catalogs, and the like, pictures dominate. Design your page in relation to the shapes and sizes of pictures you have and what you want to say about them. Are your pictures predominantly vertical, horizontal, or square? Are you presenting images only, or pictures with text?

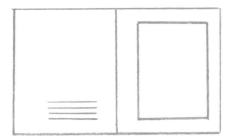

Left page for caption; right page for image. Clean separation of content and image.

Captions and pictures on the same page. This is a more cost-efficient use of space, but it also means that your pictures will most likely be smaller, to make room for captions.

BASIC PICTURE BOOKS

Pages and Spreads

Every book consists of pages that have been bound together into a sequence. When you open a book, the first page and the last page are the only ones that sit by themselves. Every other page is part of a spread—a left- and a right-hand page viewed together. Designers thus approach a book as a series of spreads, not as a series of separate pages. In a text book, the left and right sides often mirror each other. This way, the main text block is printed so that it doesn't show through from one side of the page to the other. In a picture book, images sometimes cross over from the left side to the right side of the spread. When this is the case, the designer pays attention to where the spine of the book will fall in relation to the image. The spine is a big physical and visual presence, so it shouldn't cut through important details.

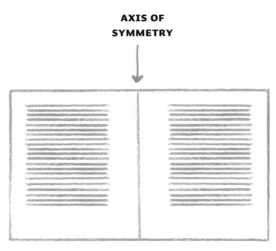

AXIS OF SYMMETRY

A SPREAD consists of a left- and a right-hand page viewed together. This is the basic unit of book design.

Table of Contents

This crucial navigation device not only tells the reader what's inside your book and where to find it, but is an important marketing tool as well. Online booksellers often feature the table of contents among the sampled pages of a book, and potential buyers use this information to decide whether to buy the book—or walk away.

LOOK INSIDE
The illustrated table of contents for *ReadyMade: How to Make (Almost) Everything* is an alluring invitation to look further. Authors, Shoshana Berger and Grace Hawthorne. Designed by Eric Heiman.

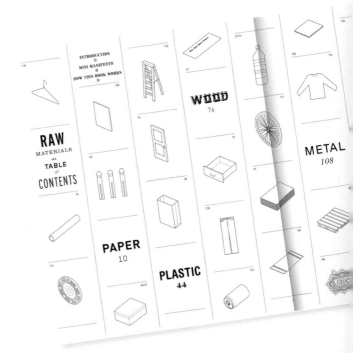

Parts of a Book

Front Matter

HALF TITLE PAGE

*full title of book,
or just the main title
if there is a lengthy
subtitle*

TITLE PAGE

*full title of book,
author, publisher, and
city of publication*

COPYRIGHT PAGE

*author, copyright,
year of publication,
ISBN, cataloging data,
publisher's address,
various credits*

TABLE OF CONTENTS

what's in the book

The half title page is luxurious, and you might choose to skip it in a more utilitarian volume such as an instruction manual or desk calendar.

Some publishers put the copyright information at the back of the book, allowing a full double-page spread for the table of contents.

Main Content

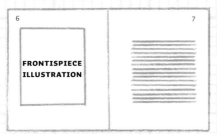

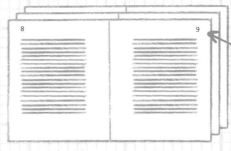

Page numbers, also called folios, appear within the margins of the book. Because every book starts with a right page, left pages are always even, and right pages are always odd.

Back Matter

APPENDICES

*these might include
glossaries, index,
checklists, biographies,
resumes, and
chronologies*

COLOPHON

*information about
typefaces, book design,
and printing or binding
techniques, if these are
of interest*

Typography

Choosing typefaces and arranging them on the pages of your book are essential steps in creating an inviting and appropriate atmosphere for your book. Designers today have a wide range of choices, including historic and contemporary fonts.

SUSTAINABLE CUISINE

those responsible for bringing the food to our plate creates a greater awareness and connection to the life-sustaining processes.

We encourage individuals to work toward grains, fruits and vegetables as a basis for their diets. Although many people cannot or will not sustain a totally vegetarian diet, we continue to work with individuals to view animal products as garnish. The individual who successfully shifts their diet to include more grains, fruits, vegetables, legumes, nuts and fewer animal products, not only greatly improves their own health, but greatly improves global health. Plant foods undeniably require fewer resources to produce and their production is healthier on our soil, water, and air. But greater benefits are gained when overall lifestyles are changed, and one becomes aware of the impact of all of their choices. Ultimately, global sustainability comes from the individual change that is, in itself, sustainable. We at the Duke Diet & Fitness Center are dedicated to helping people create and sustain lifestyle change.

28

The Power of Real Cheese

Jonathan White

Egg Farm Dairy
2 John Walsh Blvd.
Peekskill, NY 10566
www.creamery.com

For 8,000 years, there has been a triangle trade between humans, ruminants and lactic bacteria.

The humans protect and feed the livestock: sheep, cows, goats, camels, yaks, etc., while they graze on the grass and produce milk. This milk making is the result of another triangle, where the sun and soil produces grass, the cow eats the grass, and the manure fertilizes the soil.

Because the sun-grass cycle is seasonal, there is more milk in spring and less in winter. So, to balance the supply and demand, humanity developed a partnership with friendly bacteria, which ferment the surfeit spring milk into a preservable form: cheese. In subsistence agriculture, the spring milk stored as cheese

29

CLASSIC TYPOGRAPHY

The "power of cheese" is serious business for the authors of *Sustainable Cuisine White Papers*. Designer Kris Kiger has used a classic typeface to emphasize the gravitas of the subject matter. The main text block is justified (traditional), but the chapter title and author lines are set flush left (contemporary). The rounded corners and narrow page format give the book a distinctive feel. Published by Earth Pledge; distributed by Chelsea Green.

Alignment

Page layout software lets you align text in four basic ways. justified, centered, flush left, and flush right. Most books are set primarily with justified text— solid blocks that have even edges on both sides. For a novel, memoir, or other text-heavy work, justified text is the most familiar and efficient way to set the main content. You'll need to explore other forms of alignment for chapter headings, title pages, cover typography, and so on. Poetry is usually set flush left, allowing each line to break naturally as it is written, rather than being centered or forced into geometric blocks. Illustrated books are less convention-bound than text books; experiment with alignment to find what works best with your content and the point of view you hope to convey.

JUSTIFIED

This is the standard format for large bodies of text. Justified text looks neat on the page, and it is highly economical, because page layout software uses hyphenation as well as adjusting the spacing between words and letters in order to fit a maximum number of words on every line. If your line length is too short, the hyphenation and spacing will be choppy and uneven, as seen in newspapers, which often have large gaps and many hyphenated lines in a single paragraph. If you are producing your book with a word-processing program (such as Microsoft Word) instead of a full-fledged page layout program (such as InDesign), the justification can look especially bad. (Look at the line above this one.)

FLUSH LEFT

Setting text with a ragged edge along the right side of the column became common in the twentieth century. Flush left text is considered modern because it is asymmetrical and organic, allowing the flow of the language to help determine the typographic arrangement. Flush left text works well with narrower columns. The designer must pay careful attention, however, to the appearance of the rag, or the rough edge. The rag should look irregular and natural; it should not look too flat or even or form recognizable shapes such as moons, zigzags, or diving boards.

CENTERED

Static and classical, centered text is commonly used for title pages, chapter headings, and dedications.
The formal character of centered text also makes it appropriate for wedding invitations, tombstones, and the type of verse that appears inside greeting cards.
When using centered text, the designer usually breaks lines for sense, putting important words or phrases on their own lines.
Centered text often has generous line spacing.

FLUSH RIGHT

Never say never, but flush right text is rarely used for setting the entire text of a book. This setting can be highly useful, however, for creating captions, marginal notes, and other tasty typographic bits. The even right edge can be used to create a sense of affinity or magnetic attraction between different elements on the page.

Historical Book Faces

Many typefaces were created especially for use in books, including traditional fonts such as Garamond, Caslon, and Jenson, which are available today in modern digital versions that have been carefully designed to reflect their historic sources. Books can also be typeset in sans serif fonts such as Futura and Helvetica.

Jenson is based on typefaces created in the fifteenth **century by the Venetian printer Nicolas Jenson.** *Italic typefaces were created by Jenson's contemporary* LUDOVICO DEGLI ARRIGHI.

ADOBE JENSON PRO

ADOBE JENSON, designed by Robert Slimbach in 1995, expresses its Renaissance roots and yet doesn't feel mannered or precious. Look for its calligraphic origins in the ribbonlike strokes of its letters. Adobe Jenson includes SMALL CAPS as well as light, **bold**, and **semibold** weights; these weights where not used in the Renaissance. The *italics* feel especially calligraphic.

Garamond is the name for typefaces inspired by **the sixteenth-century printing fonts of Claude** *Garamond. Over the centuries, many designers have* CREATED TYPEFACES BASED ON GARAMOND'S TYPES.

ADOBE GARAMOND PRO

ADOBE GARAMOND, designed by Robert Slimbach in 1989, honors the proportions of its Renaissance source. It is less explicitly calligraphic than Jenson. Note the elegant three-dimensional bowl of the lowercase "a" and the gap in the uppercase "P." Adobe Garamond includes SMALL CAPS as well as **bold** and **semibold** weights; these weights where not used in the Renaissance. The *italics* are more lyrical than calligraphic.

Caslon is named for the British typographer **William Caslon, whose elegant and practical** *fonts were an eighteenth-century staple and a fond* PERSONAL FAVORITE OF BENJAMIN FRANKLIN.

ADOBE CASLON PRO

ADOBE CASLON was designed by Carol Twombly in 1990; it includes SMALL CAPS as well as **bold** and **semibold** weights; these weights where not used in the eighteenth century. The U.S. Declaration of Independence and the Constitution were first printed in Caslon's types. Caslon has strong vertical elements, crisp serifs, and generous, open *italics*.

Contemporary Book Faces

All around the world, graphic designers are developing new fonts and distributing them online. This book is typeset in two of the fonts displayed below, Dolly and Auto. When choosing a new typeface, look for the same book-oriented features that you would expect from a classic font, such as small capitals and non-lining numerals. You can begin to judge the quality of a typeface by how it is presented on the designer's website. Is the font displayed and described with care? Is it available in a range of weights or styles?

Dolly, the typeface used for setting the main *text of this book, was designed by Underware, an* **independent type foundry and graphic** DESIGN STUDIO IN THE NETHERLANDS.

DOLLY

DOLLY's sturdy letters are legible in small sizes, due to a relatively low contrast between thick and thin elements. Ten-point type is commonly used in books. When Dolly is applied in larger sizes, more detail becomes apparent. Dolly consists of four styles: roman, *italic*, **bold**, and SMALL CAPS, providing a healthy palette for solving basic problems of book typography.

Auto, also designed by Underware, is a sans **serif typeface. Auto is designed in several** *weights, which are used in this book for captions,* **HEADINGS, AND OTHER SUPPORTING TEXT.**

AUTO

AUTO is designed with three different italics, each with its own flavor, from simple and straightforward to curvy and sweet. Our book uses the *Auto 1 italic* set, the most neutral of the three versions. Auto is effective for headlines as well as text. The typeface features SMALL CAPS as well as light, **bold**, and **black** styles.

The Scala type family was designed by Martin *Majoor in the Netherlands in 1991. Like many* **recent typefaces, Scala is designed in both** serif and sans serif variants.

SCALA

SCALA has a classic appearance with crisp, modern details. The curves are simple, the *italics* are elegant, and the serifs consist of clean, blocky slabs. The letters have a tall x-height (the height of the lowercase body), making them legible at small sizes. It is available in both serif and sans serif versions as well as a **bold** weight.

Display Faces

In addition to typefaces intended for use in your body text, captions, subheads, and so on, you may want to add spice at larger scales with an additional typeface. Called display fonts, some faces are intended for use only as titles, headlines, logos, and other applications that involve just a few words.

THIS IS VINYL, A HOMEGROWN, HANDMADE DISPLAY FACE.

Vinyl is a typeface created by John Corrigan, one of the authors and designers of this book. This DIY typeface exists only in capital letters.

A good display face should be
CHALET

dramatic and eye-catching, yet still
BURIN SANS

READABLE. DISPLAY FACES ARE DESIGNED TO
TRADE GOTHIC

intrigue and surprise readers as well as
UNITED SERIF THIN

to deliver information. Well-chosen
FONTIN BOLD

DISPLAY FACES CAN GIVE A
HOUSE SPACEAGE ROUND

publication a distinct voice.
DOT MATRIX

SECRETS of PURGATORY PIE PRESS REVEALED!

How to MAKE BOOKS

Fold, Cut & Stitch Your Way to a One-of-a-Kind Book

ESTHER K. SMITH

LINDSAY STADIG illustrations   **DAVID MICHAEL ZIMMERMAN** photographs

BIG, STRONG TYPE

Esther K. Smith is cofounder of Purgatory Pie Press, a letterpress shop devoted to printing and making books by hand. The cover of *How to Make Books*, published by Potter Craft, features large-scale letterpress display text, set in metal type by Dikko Faust.

Cover Design

If your book is for sale, the cover is an essential marketing device that will function like a logo and advertisement. It must look great in the bookstore and on the shelf. It also has to look good when it's a tiny digital image on Amazon and other online sites.

Design Process

1. DEFINE THE PROBLEM

Write a description of what you want to say and to whom you want to say it. What's the main point of your book? What attitude do you want to express (formal, relaxed, professional, raw)? Who is your audience (friends, enemies, peers, potential employers)? Keep these goals in mind when you develop design ideas.

2. RESEARCH

Look at other books similar to yours. Think about what attracts you and note the variety of design strategies. Some covers are all type; others feature photographs and illustrations. Some are quiet; some are loud.

3. BRAINSTORM

Write down as many ideas as you can think of—good, bad, and ridiculous.

4. PRIORITIZE

Which ideas make sense with your book? Which ones are feasible for you to produce? Study your available resources, such as vintage photos or illustrations from inside the book.

5. TRY IT

If your design skills are weak, collaborate with a designer, artist, illustrator, or photographer. Look for stock images and pictures on photo sharing sites. Always respect copyrights, and keep in mind that photographs must be high-resolution and large scale to reproduce well.

6. TEST IT

Show your designs to other people for reactions. Evaluate each design. Is the title easy to read? Do the images bring attention to the title, or do they distract from it? Is there a clear hierarchy of elements? Is the design conveying the intended message and tone of voice?

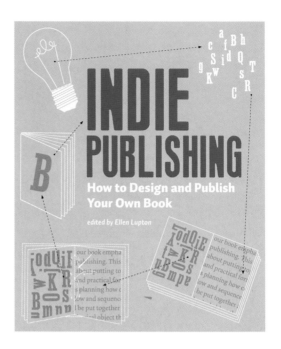

MANY VARIATIONS

Shown above is an early version of the cover that was finally chosen for this book. Designer Kelley McIntyre tried numerous color variations before finalizing the cover. This early design did not feel rich and vibrant enough. The final cover uses a background texture and more assertive colors.

TRIAL AND ERROR

A team of designers worked together to create numerous alternate covers for *Indie Publishing*. Some solutions are photographic; others use illustrations; some are purely typographic. As the team worked, they focused on their message, choosing a final design that speaks about the active, hands-on process of making a book.

Cover Gallery

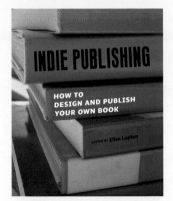

Tony Venne

Design by Ryan Clifford; illustration by Tricia Chin

Kristian Bjørnard

Joo Ha

Ryan Clifford

John Corrigan

Danielle Davis

Lindsey M. Muir

Helen Armstrong

Endpaper

In a hardcover book, the endpaper is a single sheet of paper glued to the inside of the cover and to the bound signatures. Both functional and decorative, endpapers use color and pattern to establish a mood, welcoming readers and rewarding them for opening the book. Fun and engaging endpapers are like sexy underwear for your book.

In a paperback book, you can create an effect similar to an endpaper by printing a color or pattern on the inside covers. (Check out what we did with the covers of this book.)

INSIDE STORY
The endpapers shown here (largest to smallest) are from *Hollywood Life* (designed and published by Greybull Press), *Quack Quack Quack* (designed and published by Winterhouse), and *Shortcomings* (designed by Adrian Tomine for Drawn & Quarterly).

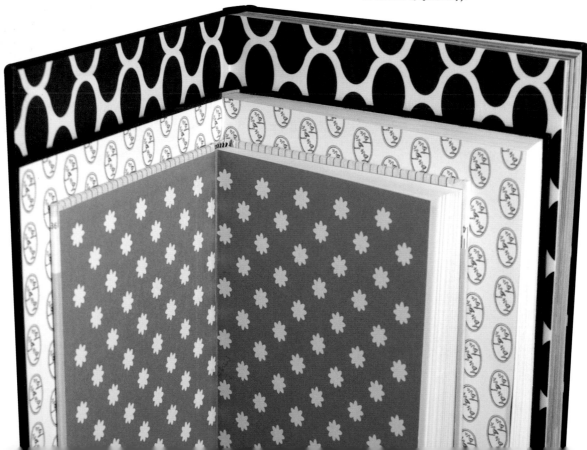

Dust Jacket

The purpose of a dust jacket is to protect the book from wear and tear. It also helps market the book and provides an additional vehicle for expression.

FANCY FLAPS When a museum in Scotland invited the radical-wallpaper designers Timorous Beasties to curate an exhibition about nature and the decorative arts, the museum wanted a deluxe and daring catalog to go with the show. The title copy repeats along the folded-back edges of the book's jacket, as if it were a length of fabric or wallpaper. Book designed by Graphic Thought Facility; published by Dundee Contemporary Arts.

InDesign Crash Course

The most efficient and effective way to design a book is using professional page layout software such as Adobe InDesign or QuarkXPress. Although it is possible, in theory, to design a book using a standard word-processing program such as Microsoft Word, doing so is frustrating and time consuming—with generally poor results. Programs like InDesign allow you to intuitively drag and drop elements as well as easily create grids, page numbers, typographic refinements, and more. The instructions here offer a brief overview of InDesign. The software's excellent Help button can answer nearly any question you have.

CREATE A NEW DOCUMENT

Check "facing pages" to create a multipage publication designed in double-page spreads. Define your document size (for example, 6 x 6 inches) so that later you can print out the document with crop marks. (When printing, select Printer Marks>Crop Marks in the print menu.) InDesign's default measurement system is picas and points; you can change this to inches or millimeters in General Preferences. Use the Columns and Margins fields to create a grid.

MAKE A TEXT FRAME

Every element in InDesign sits in a "frame" or box. To make a text frame, select the Type tool and drag it to make a frame. You can also change any frame into a text box by clicking on it with the Type tool. A cursor for text entry will appear. Use the Character window to change the typeface, size, line spacing, tracking, and other attributes. Use the Paragraph window to change alignment (flush left, flush right, centered, justified).

MAKE A PICTURE FRAME

Images sit in picture frames. Use the box tool to draw a frame. Go to File>Place to link to an illustration. InDesign creates a low-resolution preview of your illustration, allowing you to edit the image later in Photoshop or other software or to replace the picture altogether. (In contrast, Microsoft Word incorporates images directly into the document, making a massive digital file as well as limiting your editing power.) You can also crop and resize the image inside the frame without affecting the original image file.

TEXT WRAP

If a picture or text frame has a text wrap value, then text from another frame will be forced to wrap around it, rather than running on top of it or behind it. Do this with Window>Text Wrap. New objects in InDesign have no text wrap value.

HYPHENATION

Turn on automatic hyphenation when you are working with justified text. Turn it off when you are working with centered or ragged text, or with headlines of any kind. (You can always put in hyphens by hand if needed.) Click the Hyphenation box in the Paragraph tool bar.

KERNING

Adjusting the space between two letters is called *manual kerning*. (The typeface already has built-in kerning values. You are now adjusting it locally according to your own judgment.) Position your cursor between the letters you want to adjust. On a Mac, press option and the left or right arrow key to remove or add space. You will rarely need to do this unless you are working with large-scale headlines.

LOVE

These letters are set normally

LOVE

Additional space between "O" and "V"

TRACKING

Adjust letter spacing across an entire text selection (a word, line, paragraph, or more). When setting a word in all caps or small caps, for example, it is advisable to track your letters, expanding the space around them. Select the text and type in a Tracking value in the Character menu or toolbar (AV with an arrow underneath).

THIS TEXT IS ALL CAPS

Not tracked

THIS TEXT IS ALL CAPS

Tracked 100

THREADING TEXT FRAMES

You can connect two or more text frames so that text flows from one frame to another. Use this feature to create multi-column and multi-page documents. Select a text frame, and then with the white arrow tool, click the frame's in-port or out-port (little square with a plus or minus). The arrow will become a "loaded text icon." Position the loaded text icon over the frame you want to connect to. The loaded text icon becomes a thread icon. Click on the new frame to confirm the thread. Or click anywhere on the page, and InDesign will make a new frame automatically.

INSERT, DELETE, AND REARRANGE PAGES

Control pages from the Pages window. Select a page icon and delete it using the Pages options menu. Grab the page icons and move them around to reorder pages.

MASTER PAGES

A master page contains graphics that appear on every new page of a document, such as page numbers, headings, and guidelines. Select New Master from the menu behind the Pages window. Name the master and put text and other graphics on it. The master can now be applied to any or all pages. You can base a new master on an existing master, you can have several masters in one document, and you can turn an existing page into a master. For more information, see InDesign's online help.

To override master elements on a document page, press command-shift (control-shift on PC) while selecting the element. This allows you to edit or delete the item. Note that an overriden master item won't get updated on that page if you edit the master page.

For automatic page numbers, create a box and choose Type>Insert Special Character>Auto Page Number.

WORKING WITH RULES

Select Paragraph rules from the menu behind the Paragraph window. The default weight is 1 point, which looks nice on the screen but looks heavy and bland when you print it. For a clean, slim rule, choose .25 point. The Offset value controls the distance between the rule and the baseline. A rule will appear after every hard return (paragraph break). Establish rules in this way rather than "drawing" them with the line tool. This allows you to consistently control their placement and spacing.

DEFINING NEW SWATCHES

To see predefined colors that you can apply to text, rules, boxes, and so forth, open the Swatches window. Use the options menu to define new colors. Use CMYK to create mixes of cyan, magenta, yellow, and black, the colors used in standard four-color printing (as opposed to RGB: red, green, and blue, the colors of your computer screen). Avoid "spot colors" unless you are working with a commercial offset printer and you are doing a job that will use special ink colors in place of (or in addition to) standard CMYK.

Sharing Your Files

MAKE HIGH-RESOLUTION PDFS

An InDesign document can become quite complex, using numerous fonts and image links. A PDF allows you to share a high-resolution file without your printer, client, or other end user needing access to your native software or your font and image files. It's easy to make a PDF with InDesign: just hit Export>PDF. Many designers prefer to print from PDFs rather than from native InDesign files.

PREFLIGHT AND PACKAGE

Use File>Preflight to check your file for errors. The Preflight program will flag images that are RGB instead of CMYK and other problems. Use File>Package to gather up all the images and other resources used in your project. InDesign will copy all elements into a new folder.

PRINT BOOKLET

If you are producing your own stapled book or sewn signatures, File>Print Booklet rearranges your pages into "printer spreads," allowing the book to be assembled, folded, and bound together through the center. The software calculates the correct imposition of pages.

FICTION

by Kristian Bjørnard and Ellen Lupton

LEGIONS OF ASPIRING NOVELISTS LONG TO SHARE THEIR MANUSCRIPTS WITH THE WORLD. In the mainstream book industry, most editors will only look at submissions that come through a literary agent, and few agents are willing to waste their time and risk their reputations on unknown writers. Unsolicited manuscripts are sent to the "slush pile," a dumping ground periodically sifted through by low-level editorial staff. If you don't want the slush pile to be the final resting place for *your* novel, consider publishing it yourself.

The novel showcased in this chapter was written by Julia Weist, a young artist and writer. Called *Sexy Librarian*, it is a hot romance about a hip young librarian who leaves New York to work at a small-town public library in Minnesota. Kristian Bjørnard designed the cover, interior layout, and brand identity. Ellen Lupton, who took on the role of publisher, edited the novel and commissioned a prominent librarian to write a critical essay, giving the book an added layer of geeky street cred. We published *Sexy Librarian* using a print-on-demand service, a system that allows books to be digitally printed and shipped to customers one by one each time the book is ordered. The unit price for POD is higher than that for mass production, but it costs very little to get started. Your big investment will be in writing, editing, designing, and marketing your book—labors of love that take more time than money.

SEXY BOOK This book wrapped in a pair of fishnet stockings became the cover for *Sexy Librarian*. Photograph by Kristian Bjørnard.

CREATE A PRINT-ON-DEMAND BOOK IN TEN PAINSTAKING, ASS-BREAKING, MIND-NUMBING, AND TOTALLY ESSENTIAL STEPS
Follow the steps below to publish any kind of POD publication—fiction, nonfiction, poetry, exhibition catalogs, and more.

1. WRITE A BOOK That was easy!

2. CHOOSE A POD SERVICE Various services can provide you with digital printing, online distribution, and an ISBN. (Some will also design and edit the book for additional fees.) We chose to work with Lulu, a consumer-friendly service that welcomes newcomers and provides excellent support along the way. It costs nothing to upload print-ready digital files; a low fee gets you an official ISBN as well as a listing that is shared with the major internet booksellers, including Amazon, Borders, and Barnes & Noble. Books are printed and delivered one by one as customers purchase them. You set a price that includes a royalty on top of the production fee.

3. CHOOSE A FORMAT Your book's trim size or format will affect the page count as well as how the volume feels in people's hands. Maybe you want a smaller book with many pages, or a bigger book with a thinner spine. POD services are set up to produce books in a fixed number of formats as well as in hardback and paperback. Only a few trim sizes may be approved for distribution to bookstores, so choose carefully. *Sexy Librarian* is a 6-x-9-inch paperback. This size, which is larger and more elegant than a supermarket novel, gives the book the look and feel of quality fiction.

4. EDIT YOUR BOOK Every author needs an editor. If you can't afford to pay someone, find a fellow writer to help you out, someone with a firm grasp of grammar who will have the time and courage to read your novel carefully and look for errors, inconsistencies, plot glitches, and more. If you can't afford to pay this person, offer babysitting, dog walking, housekeeping, or other services in exchange.

5. DESIGN YOUR BOOK Most POD services work with PDF files, a standard document format that is generated with Adobe Acrobat Professional software. This software works with the Adobe page layout program InDesign, but it also works with Microsoft Word, QuarkXPress, and other publishing tools. You will need some software skills to produce your novel. The services of a professional graphic designer would be a big help, too; try to find one. If you can't, follow our guidelines on the following pages and keep your design as simple as possible.

6. DESIGN THE COVER A great cover is a great sales tool. If you have a design budget, here's a good place to spend it. (It turns out that many successful indie publishers happen to be married to graphic designers. Try that route, too, if you have the heart.)

7. ORDER A PROOF Read it carefully. Make corrections. Repeat. We can't stress enough the importance of the proofing process. Even if you edited your book carefully at the manuscript stage, you will find new and different errors when the pages have been typeset. Once you officially publish your book online (with that real ISBN), you are locked into the final product, and any changes you make will cost money.

8. ORDER ANOTHER PROOF Now is not the time to rush. In the mainstream publishing world, books go through many rounds of edits, and your book deserves the same care and attention. Proof your book over and over until you get it right.

9. PUBLISH YOUR BOOK When you're ready, really ready, hit the "approve" button and publish your book. That's it. It's real now.

10. MARKET YOUR BOOK Make a website. Have parties. Send out review copies. Call up local bookstores. Arrange readings at bars, libraries, community centers, gas stations—anywhere you can find an audience. No one will read your book unless you tell them about it. Even a book produced by a mainstream publisher depends on endless love and energy from its author to get the word out. Love your book, and do not let it die.

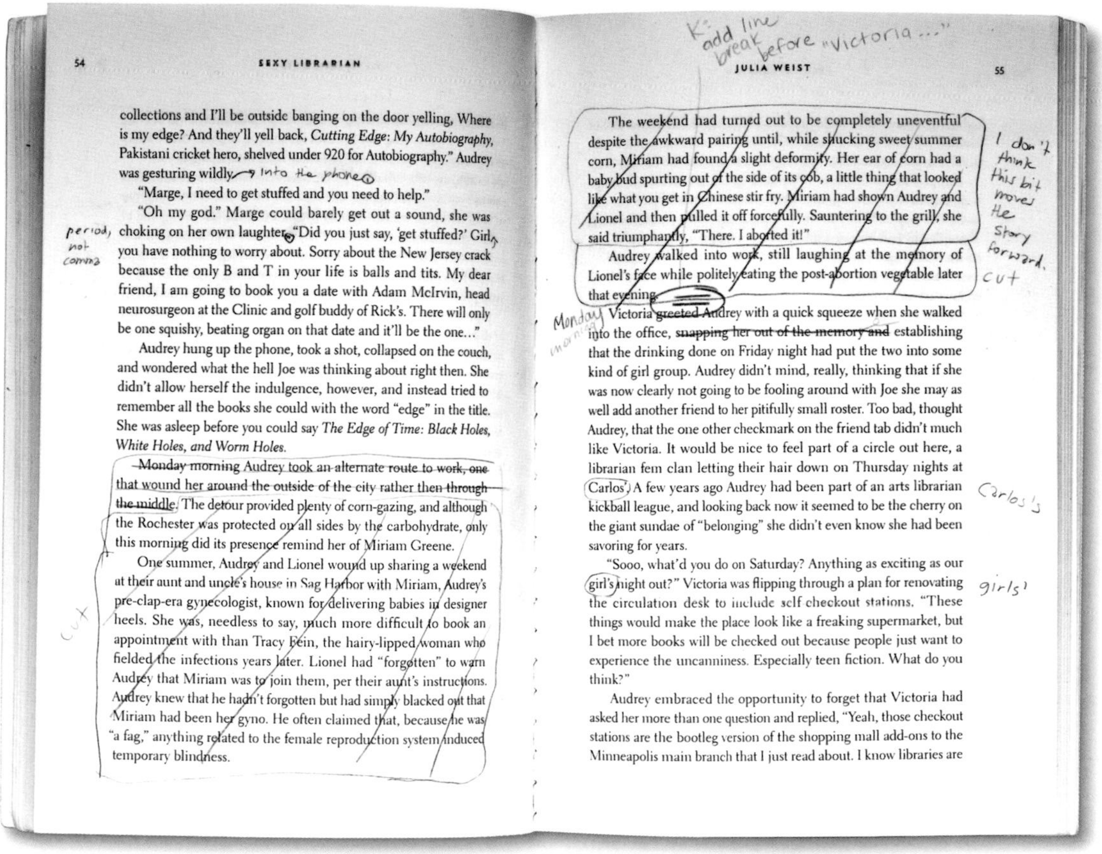

collections and I'll be outside banging on the door yelling, *Where is my edge?* And they'll yell back, *Cutting Edge: My Autobiography*, Pakistani cricket hero, shelved under 920 for Autobiography." Audrey was gesturing wildly. [into the phone]

"Marge, I need to get stuffed and you need to help."

"Oh my god." Marge could barely get out a sound, she was choking on her own laughter. "Did you just say, 'get stuffed?' Girl, you have nothing to worry about. Sorry about the New Jersey crack because the only B and T in your life is balls and tits. My dear friend, I am going to book you a date with Adam McIrvin, head neurosurgeon at the Clinic and golf buddy of Rick's. There will only be one squishy, beating organ on that date and it'll be the one…"

Audrey hung up the phone, took a shot, collapsed on the couch, and wondered what the hell Joe was thinking about right then. She didn't allow herself the indulgence, however, and instead tried to remember all the books she could with the word "edge" in the title. She was asleep before you could say *The Edge of Time: Black Holes, White Holes, and Worm Holes.*

Monday morning Audrey took an alternate route to work, one that wound her around the outside of the city rather then through the middle. The detour provided plenty of corn-gazing, and although the Rochester was protected on all sides by the carbohydrate, only this morning did its presence remind her of Miriam Greene.

One summer, Audrey and Lionel wound up sharing a weekend at their aunt and uncle's house in Sag Harbor with Miriam, Audrey's pre-clap-era gynecologist, known for delivering babies in designer heels. She was, needless to say, much more difficult to book an appointment with than Tracy Fein, the hairy-lipped woman who fielded the infections years later. Lionel had "forgotten" to warn Audrey that Miriam was to join them, per their aunt's instructions. Audrey knew that he hadn't forgotten but had simply blacked out that Miriam had been her gyno. He often claimed that, because he was "a fag," anything related to the female reproductive system induced temporary blindness.

[margin annotations: period, not coming; cut]

[annotation: K — add line break before "Victoria…"]

The weekend had turned out to be completely uneventful despite the awkward pairing until, while shucking sweet summer corn, Miriam had found a slight deformity. Her ear of corn had a baby bud sputting out of the side of its cob, a little thing that looked like what you get in Chinese stir fry. Miriam had shown Audrey and Lionel and then pulled it off forcefully. Sauntering to the grill, she said triumphantly, "There. I aborted it!"

Audrey walked into work, still laughing at the memory of Lionel's face while politely eating the post-abortion vegetable later that evening.

[annotation: Monday (morning)] Victoria greeted Audrey with a quick squeeze when she walked into the office, snapping her out of the memory and establishing that the drinking done on Friday night had put the two into some kind of girl group. Audrey didn't mind, really, thinking that if she was now clearly not going to be fooling around with Joe she may as well add another friend to her pitifully small roster. Too bad, thought Audrey, that the one other checkmark on the friend tab didn't much like Victoria. It would be nice to feel part of a circle out here, a librarian fem clan letting their hair down on Thursday nights at Carlos'. A few years ago Audrey had been part of an arts librarian kickball league, and looking back now it seemed to be the cherry on the giant sundae of "belonging" she didn't even know she had been savoring for years.

"Sooo, what'd you do on Saturday? Anything as exciting as our girl's night out?" Victoria was flipping through a plan for renovating the circulation desk to include self checkout stations. "These things would make the place look like a freaking supermarket, but I bet more books will be checked out because people just want to experience the uncanniness. Especially teen fiction. What do you think?"

Audrey embraced the opportunity to forget that Victoria had asked her more than one question and replied, "Yeah, those checkout stations are the bootleg version of the shopping mall add-ons to the Minneapolis main branch that I just read about. I know libraries are

[margin annotations: I don't think this bit moves the story forward. cut; Carlos's; girls']

THE PROOF IS IN THE PUDDING

We ordered five waves of proofs before publishing the final version. We focused on the text during the first two rounds, and then we concentrated on the cover in the final rounds, honing the concept and tweaking the photography. The editor, designer, and author played a role at every stage. Photos by Dan Meyers.

Front Matter

The front matter includes the parts of a book that precede the actual contents, including the title page, copyright page, and table of contents. Sometimes a preface, acknowledgment, or dedication is included in this section as well. The front matter introduces your book and sets the visual atmosphere, like bringing flowers to a dinner date. The front matter also includes essential publishing data about your book. (See more in "Publishing Basics.")

TITLE PAGE shows the full title of the book and lists the author as well as special contributors. The title page also lists the publisher and the city of publication.

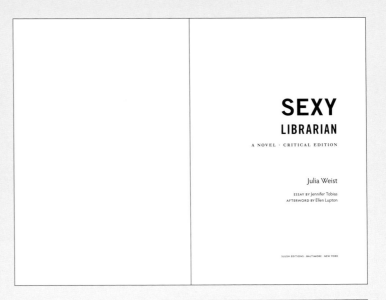

COPYRIGHT PAGE typically appears on the back of the title page. It provides details such as the publisher's address and website, copyright date, and the ever-crucial ISBN. Also valuable is cataloging information for libraries; our book includes a custom catalog record written by Sherman Clarke, a prominent librarian.

TABLE OF CONTENTS is a menu for your book. A novel doesn't necessarily need one, but since our book includes critical essays, it was essential.

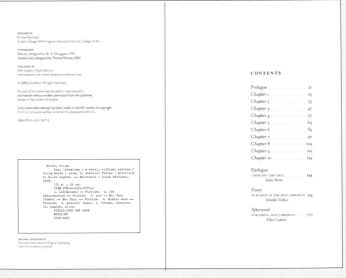

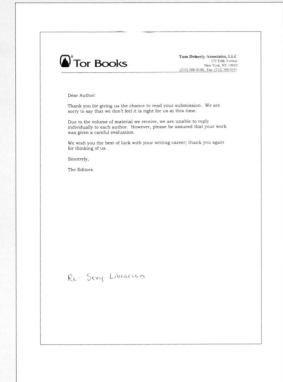

Unique Enterprises-Submissions <uniqueenterprisessubmit@yahoo.com>   Thu, Oct 26, 2006
To: Julia Weist <juliaweist@gmail.com>   at 1:37 AM

Dear Julia,

Thank you for thinking of Moonlit Romance and allowing us to review the sample chapters of
Sexy Librarian. Unfortunately, this manuscript does not meet our needs at this time. We require that
the main protagonists maintain a monogamous relationship, and to preserve the 'fantasy' factor of the
romance novel, we currently do not publish novels which include STDs. We have found that
emphasizing safe sex in practice is more acceptable to our readership than mentioning diseases
which tend to turn off our readers. Again, thank you for considering Moonlit Romance, and we wish
you the best of luck in placing your manuscript elsewhere.

Yours,
Editorial Staff
Moonlit Romance and Moonlit Madness

FIRST COMES REJECTION *Sexy Librarian* starts out with Julia Weist's initial rejection letters from commercial romance publishers. The letters provide a fascinating glimpse into the harsh world of publishing. It's undeniably titillating to witness someone else's rejection. The standard order and content of the front matter picks up after the rejection letters: title page, copyright page, and table of contents.

Page Layout

A typical mass-market paperback has as much text as possible shoveled onto every page. More luxurious editions use more white space (yielding a higher page count and a higher price for printing, paper, and binding). Designer Kristian Bjørnard tested several layouts for *Sexy Librarian* before choosing one that felt just right.

DRAB LAYOUT

This plain-vanilla design features narrow margins, which save space. But since *Sexy Librarian* is a fairly short novel, we actually wanted to beef up the page count; more generously designed layouts would yield a heftier book in the end. Making any book format symmetrical (with margins mirroring each other from left to right) prevents the block of text from showing through on the other side.

DELUXE LAYOUT

The text block in this format follows the ratio of the Golden Section (1 : 1.618 or a : b = b (a + b). Architects, painters, and book designers have used this classical system of proportion for hundreds of years. Although the layout shown here may have worked well for a treatise on wine tasting or coin collecting, it seemed too pretentious and grandiose for *Sexy Librarian*.

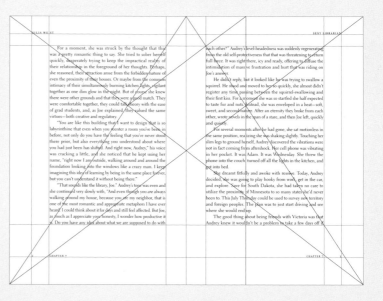

2   SEXY LIBRARIAN

Running Heads and page numbers
(in Hypatia Sans)

1 Hypatia Sans

body copy, Electra

to interact with men with whom she had no chance of sleeping. The significantly older gentlemen, celebrities, the live-in fiancés of other girls, the men who are not normally characterized as potential sexual partners, were for some reason under a different classification for Audrey. She was, after all, a librarian, and it was her job to categorize the true character of things by the most specific criteria. William, her ex and first college love, currently living with his girlfriend in Greenpoint, was not filed under "unavailable," but rather "usually occupied."

One can imagine, therefore, that when Audrey transmitted to Will the aforementioned power couple of vaginal dysfunction, things got a little complicated. When the girlfriend acquired the surprises and yet nonetheless continued her romantic and domestic partnership with Will, things got a little confusing. When Will explained to Audrey in their final conversation that neither he nor said girlfriend could afford a New York one-bedroom that wasn't shared by two people and decided it would be easier to forgive and forget than endure such a drastic change in lifestyle, Audrey knew she had to take a vacation.

The second incident was, quite simply, a "not-boyfriend" becoming a "live-in boyfriend" following the loss of his irregular installation job at PS1. After "just crashing" for three weeks, Jacob, a one-time football star turned abstract painter, discovered that selling coke was an easier way to make money than part-time museum work, and left way more time for his canvases. As the paintings were stacking up and Audrey's socks were disappearing, she knew it was time to move. Out of the city, away from the bad choices and lost nights, to a place where after working hundred-hour weeks between the library and her studio, she could be bone tired somewhere that was not always too noisy to sleep deeply.

That place, as it turned out, was Rochester, Minnesota. Thanks to the Mayo Clinic, the nation's best and largest hospital, this was where patients went hoping for some miracle to keep them from dying. To Audrey, the position of head librarian for the Arts Collection opening that May was just what the doctor ordered.

Audrey was tall, lithe, and super sexy. She was sitting at her new desk, getting to know the holdings of the Rochester Public Library's collection, a task she regarded as one of the most insignificant undertakings of her last ten years. Quickly and silently admonishing herself for being so geocentric—defining irrelevant as land-locked—Audrey tried to remind herself that this was a time for emotional growth. She pressed a finger to her thick, black, Prada glasses, rubbed her legs together lazily, and wrote on a stray card catalog card: "Be less pretentious." It was the first, and only, personal touch she had made to her work space. The adjacent desk boasted a photo of a Jell-O mold used to form the words "Number One Grandma," and Audrey hastily discarded the note, lest she appear insincere.

The last week had been hazy and automatic, as she set about to close up her life in New York like a widow in an interstitial phase of grief: numb and productive. She was worried only about leaving behind her books, now under the charge of a subletter, and about people talking to her out here like she was some kind of alien. The woman at the Java Hut this morning glanced at Audrey's designer T-shirt,

SEXY LAYOUT

The final page layout for *Sexy Librarian* features margins that are generous but not too generous. The centered heads provide a classical feeling, but the overall design is not over-the-top elegant. The book is friendly, readable, and approachable—like a girl you might say hello to in a bar.

Typography

Literary works are usually set in traditional serif typefaces, such as Garamond, Caslon, and Sabon. (See "Design Basics.") For the main text of *Sexy Librarian* we used a clean but classical typeface called Electra, designed by W. A. Dwiggins in 1935. The running heads, chapter numbers, and other supporting elements are set in Hypatia, designed by Thomas Phinney in 2007; this crisp, contemporary sans serif font retains some of the handwritten qualities of traditional typefaces. It provides a nice complement to Electra.

Designers often choose a different font altogether for a book's cover, where specific qualities may be needed to work with the chosen imagery as well as to achieve high impact at the point of purchase.

Cover Design

The cover of your novel is the first thing a potential reader will see. This essential marketing tool needs to speak loudly and clearly from a bookstore shelf or an online sales site, catching attention and conveying ideas in a direct and powerful way. The cover will become a kind of logo for your book, appearing at a tiny scale in book reviews and press announcements as well as full sized on the front of your actual novel. Good book covers help sell books and make them memorable. They entice readers to pick up the book and look inside.

To create the cover for *Sexy Librarian*, designer Kristian Bjørnard developed half a dozen different design directions to share with the author. (Unless an author is a household name, a commercial publisher will rarely allow him or her to comment on cover designs.) A pictorial solution seemed appropriate for this novel, so in order to prototype a number of design concepts quickly, Kristian researched images on the internet and took a number of shots himself, keeping in mind that he would need to acquire rights to or produce high-quality images later. Most of Kristian's initial designs conveyed the book's sexy, tongue-in-cheek attitude by playing with clichés about librarians or suggesting love in the stacks.

The author was most intrigued by a design featuring not a cute librarian but an old-fashioned card catalog card embellished with a lipstick kiss. "Fetishize the *book*, not the librarian," she suggested. "Make the book into the sexy object." In the next set of designs, Kristian dressed up a blank book in various articles of sexy lingerie, and he tried various ways to integrate the title with the photographs. The final cover is startlingly simple: a basic book is wearing fishnet stockings, with the text set big and bold over the photograph. The cover resulted from a successful dialog between author and designer—something that seldom takes place within mainstream publishing.

TYPE AND IMAGE
The title of your book doesn't have to be huge, but it does have to stand out. Integrating the title with a background picture can be tricky. If the picture has a lot of variation in color and contrast, then the letterforms will start to disappear against parts of the image. In this design, a thin white outline around the letters helps separate the text from the photograph. Next time you are at a bookstore, look at the different ways designers handle this problem. The easiest solution is to start with a photograph that has big areas of simple, nearly solid tone; the photograph used here was especially hard to work with. Photo by Paul Bradbury.

PROGRESSION

Often, an initial idea will spark a new direction. One of the early cover proposals for *Sexy Librarian* featured an image of an old catalog card embellished with a lipstick kiss. After seeing this version, the author got new ideas about where the design could go. She encouraged designer Kristian Bjørnard to experiment with "sexy books" (instead of picturing the actual librarian). The cover progressed through various stages of costume before reaching its final state: a simple white book wrapped in a fishnet stocking.

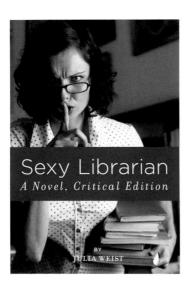

THE REFUSE PILE

Plenty of designs get scrapped along the way due to differing opinions and desires among authors, designers, and publishers. The author didn't want to see a librarian on the cover.

AND THE WINNER IS...

The final cover design for *Sexy Librarian*, shown above, is powerful and direct, with no distracting elements. Getting to that point required multiple photo shoots and design studies. Design and photography by Kristian Bjørnard.

Promotion and Marketing

Now that your book is published, it's time to get it out there. A website will be your most valuable tool. Use it to reach potential readers as well as journalists and bloggers who want easy access to excerpts, author photos, and cover art. The website for *Sexy Librarian* includes a news blog feature for documenting special events and publicity. Create a press release to send out with review copies and to distribute online, and come up with fun promotional materials such as postcards, bookmarks, T-shirts, and mugs to share at parties and special events.

Your book is more than an end in itself: it's about you or your organization. Even if a self-published book does not sell a huge number of copies, it can bring attention to your work as an artist, writer, or expert commentator. Forget advertising. It's expensive and far less effective than press notices and word of mouth. Do your research and reach out to likely editors with a short, crisp email and a link to your website. Send them a book if they express interest.

SEXY BRAND

The website for *Sexy Librarian* was built with open source custom blogging software (Textpattern). If you have minimal tech skills, use Blogger, MySpace, or Facebook to promote your book. Employ visual elements from your book cover to reinforce the image of your project. The brand imagery for *Sexy Librarian* is drawn from the book's back cover.

ELLEN LUPTON / SLUSH EDITIONS

FOR IMMEDIATE RELEASE
January 15, 2008

CONTACT:
www.sexylibrariannovel.com

JULIA WEIST'S FIRST NOVEL IS A ROMANCE, A SCULPTURE, AND AN EXPERIMENT IN INDEPENDENT PUBLISHING

Julia Weist's novel *Sexy Librarian* is a romance about a young, hyper-sophisticated librarian who leaves New York City for a job at a small-town public library. *Sexy Librarian* began as an installation at Cooper Union School of Art in New York City. While studying the deaccession policies of public libraries (and working herself in a small-town library), Weist learned that romance novels have the shortest shelf life of any category of popular fiction. After reading dozens of discarded romances, Weist decided to write her own love story. Following industry guidelines, she wrote sample chapters and sent her proposal to half a dozen major romance publishers, all of whom rejected it. She exhibited the rejection letters as a work of art.

Those letters inspired writer and curator Ellen Lupton, an advocate of DIY design and independent media, to publish *Sexy Librarian*. "Why are books rejected?" asks Lupton. "The modern publishing industry is a system of gateways that limit the entrance of newcomers. Today, that is changing as creative producers in every field are by-passing the gatekeepers and producing their own work." *Sexy Librarian* is published using print-on-demand technology (POD), which allows a book to be digitally printed one by one upon the point of purchase, sidestepping the old laws of mass production. The book is sold online for $15 a copy, http://www.SexyLibrarianNovel.com.

Published as a critical edition, *Sexy Librarian* includes an essay by renowned librarian Jennifer Tobias, a witty account of the librarian's changing image as a figure of erotic repression and possibility. "Nineteenth-century librarians were wrong to think that sexuality could be removed from the workplace," writes Tobias, "but they were right to believe that it shouldn't matter." The book also includes Weist's account of her broader artist

— MORE —

DESIGN: KRISTIAN BJØRNARD

SEXY PRESS RELEASE Develop a press release that tells a story about your book. Thousands of romances are published each year, but *Sexy Librarian* is more than a romance. It's an experimental project that speaks to specific audiences such as artists, librarians, designers, and aspiring publishers. Using this hook, we were able to get press in publications such as *ReadyMade* magazine and the *New York Sun*.

Marketing Tips

IT'S NOT JUST ABOUT THE BOOK
Many successful authors get more out of the side-opportunities associated with their books than from actually selling copies. Use your book to attract publicity, gigs, speaking engagements, consultant work, radio appearances, and more.

BROADEN YOUR NOTION OF SUCCESS
Don't use book sales as a measure of success; instead, gauge how much attention or the number of new opportunities the book has brought you. (Personal satisfaction counts, too!)

HAVE A HOOK
Authors tend to promote the "book itself" to potential media venues, when instead they should pitch a "story" revolving around the author, the subject matter, or a special audience.

FOCUS ON YOUR MARKET
Most books will appeal to certain niches (graphic designers, gay nurses, tattoo artists, born-again vegans, etc.). There's more to be gained from speaking to your community than reaching out too broadly and watering down your message.

DON'T LOSE STEAM
Authors tend to get fatigued after a month or two. Keep up the activity.

More Indie Fiction

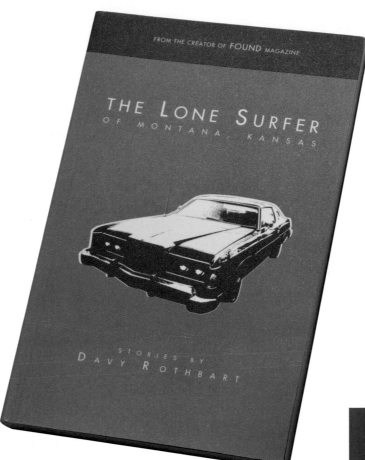

FROM INDIE TITLE TO MASS MARKETPLACE

Many indie authors dream of their short-run novels getting picked up by a mainstream publisher. Davy Rothbart self-published his chillingly honest collection of short stories in an edition of 3,000, designed by his friend Paul Hornschemeier. Davy sold the book informally as he toured the country reading from his indie zine *Found*. Wherever he went, he encouraged local bookstores to carry the book. *The Lone Surfer* was soon acquired by an editor at Simon & Schuster. The trade edition has a new cover (right) that punches up the look of the indie original (top). Photo by Dan Meyers.

THINK SMALL

The editions shown here take a hardcore DIY approach. Photocopied and stapled together like simple zines, books like these are produced in small runs and sold locally and at zine fairs, online, and at specialty bookstores. *Angell of Death* (left) has a screen-printed cover and photocopied interior; published by FROMTHEFACTORY Press; fiction by Charlie Angell; art by Nathan Danilowicz. Shown below, cover and spread from two issues of *Inch*, which measures 4.25 x 5.5 inches. Published by Bull City Press; microfiction by Michael McFee. Photos by Dan Meyers.

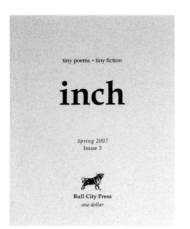

tiny poems · tiny fiction

inch

Spring 2007
Issue 3

Bull City Press
one dollar

Two Stories by Michael McFee

THE GREEN BLOUSE

At lunch, after pinot grigios, the woman drops olive oil onto her new linen blouse, a dark nipple-spot she dabs at with a damp napkin. But the stain stays when the fabric dries.

So once they get back to his place, he says *Let me wash your blouse*, hoping she'll just take it off and hand it to him, and then the rest of her clothes will follow; but instead she changes in his bedroom and hands it out the door and borrows a big t-shirt while he starts the machine.

After black coffees, he hangs it on the line: while the sun does its job, they talk for hours about her dead pets and kin and long-range plans. She sits on the counter, on the couch, in his leather desk chair: subtly he tries to touch her, but she always remains barely out of reach, a clever magnet repelled just so.

When they go outside and unpin the blouse, the stain is gone, though now the green is wrinkled as lettuce. So he says *Let me iron this for you*, and does, in the dusky kitchen, while she tells him cheerfully sad stories about her most recent lovers. Linen takes the hottest setting.

Changed again, she waves goodbye. He watches her go, knowing this is the closest he'll ever get to the smooth dream of her skin: the green blouse itself, still unwrinkled, still damply warm, half-hugging her body on its way to somebody else.

BABY, IT'S COLD OUTSIDE

"How bout some X-mas cheer?" he asked, heaving heavy cardboard boxes onto the counter. I hadn't seen him since his wife drove off months ago: he was all stubble and holey sweater and cuff-frayed cords.

"Vintage stuff," he said, patting the albums, and I knew without looking what they were: hundreds of holiday records he'd bought (many from me) for the sake of a single kitschy track, "Merry Twist-mas" or "Santa Claus Got Stuck in My Chimney" or "Shouldn't Have Given Him a Gun for Christmas," songs he'd copy onto his annual seasonal mix tapes. At first they were fun, clever and quirky like him, welcome antidotes to schmaltz, but they grew so weird and dark that people listened to them uneasily, if at all.

I flipped past "Disco Yule," "The Chipmunks' Noel," "A Pat Boone Christmas," and all the other dank LPs, once brand-new inside cellophane and jackets and sleeves, ready to set a festive mood. Then I said what he must have known I'd say: "Sorry, man, I can't use any of these." Who'd buy them but him anyhow?

"Well then," he said, "got a dumpster?" And so we walked out back, and stacked up the boxes from the counter and his trunk, and started tossing all that pressed and packaged merriment into the mostly-empty bin, caroling as vinyl cracked against metal, cheering if covers slipped off and flew into the parking lot, a couple of anti-Santas lightening their load on a bitter February afternoon.

...nd so I plod, plod, plod

...e still left (or else bereft)

...always leaning toward / d...

...the right one. Can't you...

POETRY

by Jeremy Botts

WHILE A TRIP TO THE POETRY SHELF AT BARNES & NOBLE OR ANOTHER MEGABOOKSELLER will turn up mostly books by dead authors and major literary prize winners, poetry is a living form of expression that finds its way into print via the devoted efforts of countless small presses and indie producers.

Chapbooks have been around almost as long as the printing press. They originated as cheaply bound, roughly printed pamphlets that were carried around from village to village by a "chapman," a kind of peddler. Consisting of a dozen or so pages, these early chapbooks were informal, underground publications filled with bawdy stories and simple poems. In the nineteenth century, the fine press movement revived the idea of the chapbook as a way to publish small, collectible editions in a pamphlet form (typically one or two sewn signatures).

Today, chapbooks and single-sheet broadsides are a vital part of the independent publishing movement. A modern chapbook is a bound edition of poetry, generally containing forty or fewer poems, printed in a small edition for limited distribution. Many literary magazines and poetry organizations sponsor chapbook competitions that result in the publication of a poet's work. You can also make and distribute your own chapbook.

LETTERPRESS BROADSIDE

A broadside is a single-sheet publication, sometimes folded, created for display in public places. Today, poets, artists, and designers sometimes use the broadside as an intimate and elegant form of unbound publication. Like the chapbook, the broadside is a commercial format that has evolved into an artistic medium. "Entreaty to Decision," by Sharon Dolin. Printed by Delphi Basilicato for the Center for Book Arts.

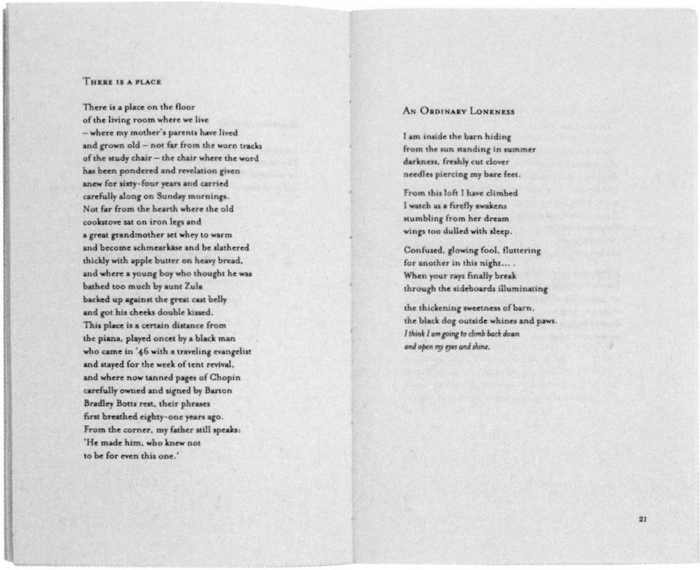

THERE IS A PLACE

There is a place on the floor
of the living room where we live
– where my mother's parents have lived
and grown old – not far from the worn tracks
of the study chair – the chair where the word
has been pondered and revelation given
anew for sixty-four years and carried
carefully along on Sunday mornings.
Not far from the hearth where the old
cookstove sat on iron legs and
a great grandmother set whey to warm
and become schmearkase and be slathered
thickly with apple butter on heavy bread,
and where a young boy who thought he was
bathed too much by aunt Zula
backed up against the great cast belly
and got his cheeks double kissed.
This place is a certain distance from
the piana, played oncet by a black man
who came in '46 with a traveling evangelist
and stayed for the week of tent revival,
and where now tanned pages of Chopin
carefully owned and signed by Barton
Bradley Botts rest, their phrases
first breathed eighty-one years ago.
From the corner, my father still speaks:
'He made him, who knew not
to be for even this one.'

AN ORDINARY LONENESS

I am inside the barn hiding
from the sun standing in summer
darkness, freshly cut clover
needles piercing my bare feet.

From this loft I have climbed
I watch as a firefly awakens
stumbling from her dream
wings too dulled with sleep.

Confused, glowing fool, fluttering
for another in this night... .
When your rays finally break
through the sideboards illuminating

the thickening sweetness of barn,
the black dog outside whines and paws.
*I think I am going to climb back down
and open my eyes and shine.*

21

Chapbooks are produced in many ways. They can be exquisitely crafted objects, printed via letterpress on fine paper, or they can be reproduced on a photocopier and bound together with staples. Flat sheets called broadsides are another format option. Poetry societies and literary magazines issue chapbooks produced via offset printing as well as letterpress. Some are luxuriously produced; others are simple and utilitarian. Poets often include illustrations in their chapbooks, featuring their own work or that of another artist. A chapbook can be a collaboration among a poet, illustrator, and master printer or designer.

The chapbook shown here, called *This Placement*, was handmade using a combination of desktop printing and traditional bookmaking techniques. (Learn more about these and other binding methods in the "Make Your Own Books" section of this volume.) *This Placement* was published in an edition of 150. The chapbooks were distributed informally among friends and left in local cafes and coffee houses for people to discover and enjoy.

THIS PLACEMENT
This saddle-stitched handmade chapbook is coauthored by Jeremy Botts and Bryce Alan Flurie; designed by Jeremy Botts.

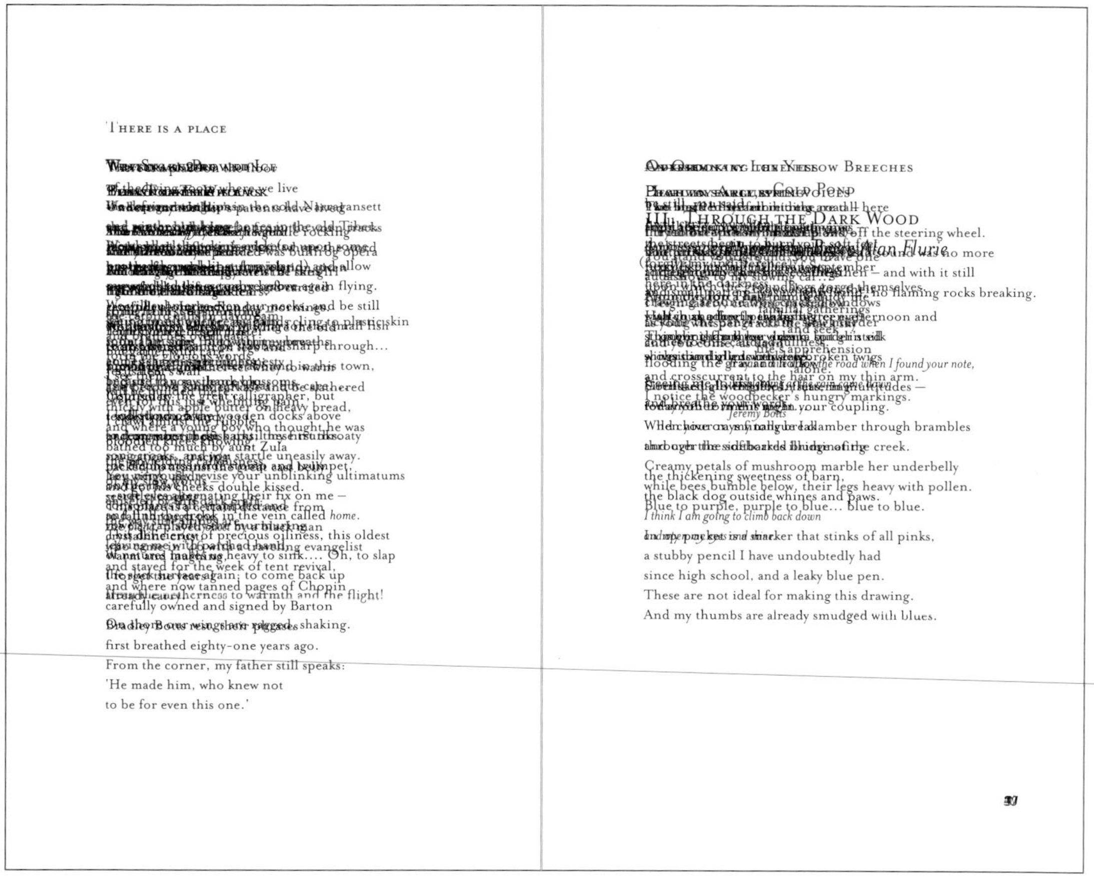

THERE IS A PLACE

[overlapping text, largely illegible] ...we live
...Narragansett
...the old...
...hollow
...flying.
...be still
...his skin
...through...
...in his town.
...weathered
...on heavy bread,
...wooden docks above
...who thought he was
...soaty
...by aunt Zula
...startle uneasily away.
...and trumpet.
...your unblinking ultimatums
...double kissed.
...their fix on me —
...mate from
...in the vein called *home*.
...of precious oiliness, this oldest
...evangelist
...heavy to sink.... Oh, to slap
...the week of tent revival,
...again; to come back up
...tanned pages of Chopin
...and the flight!
...carefully owned and signed by Barton

...shaking.
first breathed eighty-one years ago.

From the corner, my father still speaks:
'He made him, who knew not
to be for even this one.'

[right column overlapping text, largely illegible]

...BREECHES

...Gregory...

III THROUGH THE DARK WOOD

Man Elune

...off the steering wheel.
...no more
...— and with it still
...to flaming rocks breaking.
...afternoon and
...apprehension
...broken twigs
...the road when I found your note,
...to the hair on my thin arm.
...woodpecker's hungry markings
...your coupling.
Jeremy Bass

...amber through brambles
...bridge of the creek.

Creamy petals of mushroom marble her underbelly
the thickening sweetness of barn,
while bees bumble below, their legs heavy with pollen.
the black dog outside whines and paws.
Blue to purple, purple to blue... blue to blue.
I think I am going to climb back down

...darker that stinks of all pinks,
a stubby pencil I have undoubtedly had
since high school, and a leaky blue pen.
These are not ideal for making this drawing.
And my thumbs are already smudged with blues.

TYPOGRAPHY

To make your poetry sit with ease and authority on the page, you will want pay close attention to typography. Line breaks are often important to the reading of a poem, so choose a typeface and size that will accommodate your longest line and longest poem comfortably. Typefaces have distinct qualities; a traditional book face might allow the voice and content of your poems to speak most clearly. Placing your poems on the page can give them a specific feel as well. In *This Placement*, each poem is optically centered on the page. The diagram above shows the accumulated weight of the poems over the course of the entire book. The book was designed in a professional page layout program (InDesign); it was output via laser printer onto archival paper. After the books were bound, the pages were trimmed slightly narrower than 8.5 x 11 to give the book a less ordinary and utilitarian feel.

THISPLACEMENT
new work by Jeremy Botts & Bryce Alan Flurie

FIAMMASCURA PRESS   Lewisberry   2000

CONTENTS

STANDING AS SHAG HICKORY

Disheveled as
the flaking bark,
chapped by a raging wind.
Stolid in rooted thisplacement,
living with this ancient soil,
in this elderly air, graven
with thick sadnesses.

Glow dissonance echoes, cracked
like the beckoning temple bell....

The trees have no concern
for our acts, or our deep
imagined kinship with them.
Nor fields and grasses our names,
our callings.... But we wake
at these dark joys, to our oblivious
impermanence.

Jeremy Botts and Bryce Alan Flurie

I. THE BEGINNING AND AN ENDING
by Bryce Alan Flurie

"Our very existence is subsistence in God alone."
John Calvin

THE BEGINNING

Day One   Nothing.
Less than empty,
what we know as
earth with out
substance. Then a
command. The first sentence
uttered created the
first separation.
Day – light.
Dark – night
Evolving into
dawn, twilight,
dusk as the
ephemeral essence advances
across the
earth's plane.

Day Two   Space.
What miraculous paradox, to
create the boundless
expanse of sky.
The divine architect
forming necessary emptiness
from nothing.
Could this also be an introduction
of gravity? A region of
nullity, separating
the waters and keeping
them in place.

5

THE WOODS ARE EMPTY

The woods are empty today
even though I walk within.
A presence is starkly lacking
though it beckons
through the fields
nor fallow yet barren.

Shag hickory lacks its rustic
charm. The stream trickles in
silence, and mud is thicker,
and the sun is hotter,
the breeze harder
now in this hollow farm.

Grasses cut, fields planted
yet the trees desire more
even though I'm walking, weeping in
clothes come through more than
one hundred times before.

MY WISE SISTERS AND BROTHER

My wise sisters and brother
you know
more than I.
A broken, faceless
angel guards you.
You know our parents
intimately in ways
beyond my ability
to perceive.
You've watched as
decades pass,
kingdoms fell,
and as new members
added to the family
grow to adulthood.
And above all this,
you know our
father better than
even our mother.

Oh, collected siblings with less
than a day of life
between you,
you know the awareness
life cannot bring and
you know death's inherent
knowledge, the
awareness found
beyond existence.

With aching ears from
the pounding of God's silence,
I sit, pushing back the
shadows, realizing you
know more than I.

9

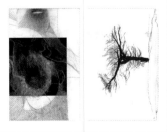

SEQUENCE

Thumbnails allow you to view your
entire book in sequence, from the title
page to a closing statement. Be sure
your book has a defined beginning
and end.

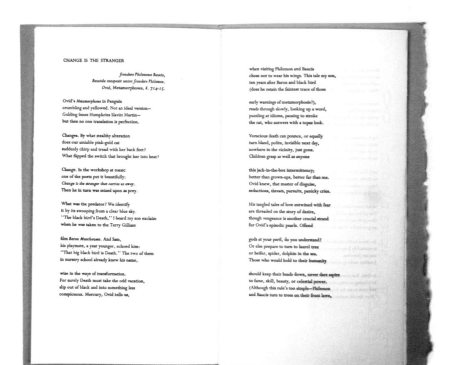

POETRY MEETS FINE PRINTING

The Center for Book Arts in New York City is a not-for-profit arts institution dedicated to preserving the traditions of bookmaking as well as exploring new approaches to the book as an art object. The CBA has an annual chapbook competition that pairs poets with designers and printers. Above and right, *Two Poems*, pamphlet-stitched letterpress chapbook by Rachel Hadas; designed and printed by Barry Magid.

Cinnamon Bay Sonnets, stab-bound letterpress chapbook written by Andrew Kaufman; designed by Barry Magid, Dim Gray Bar Press; printed by interns at the CBA under the direction of Russell Maret.

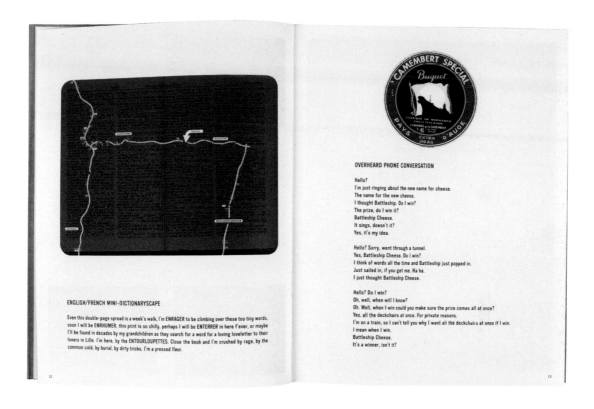

ENGLISH/FRENCH MINI-DICTIONARYSCAPE

Even this double-page spread is a week's walk, I'm ENRAGER to be climbing over these too tiny words, soon I will be ENRHUMER, this print is so chilly, perhaps I will be ENTERRER in here f'ever, or maybe I'll be found in decades by my grandchildren as they search for a word for a loving loveletter to their lovers in Lille. I'm here, by the ENTOURLOUPETTES. Close the book and I'm crushed by rage, by the common cold, by burial, by dirty tricks. I'm a pressed fleur.

OVERHEARD PHONE CONVERSATION

Hello?
I'm just ringing about the new name for cheese.
The name for the new cheese.
I thought Battleship. Do I win?
The prize, do I win it?
Battleship Cheese.
It sings, doesn't it?
Yes, it's my idea.

Hello? Sorry, went through a tunnel.
Yes, Battleship Cheese. Do I win?
I think of words all the time and Battleship just popped in.
Just sailed in, if you get me. Ha ha.
I just thought Battleship Cheese.

Hello? Do I win?
Oh, well, when will I know?
Oh. Well, when I win could you make sure the prize comes all at once?
Yes, all the deckchairs at once. For private reasons.
I'm on a train, so I can't tell you why I want all the deckchairs at once if I win.
I mean when I win.
Battleship Cheese.
It's a winner, isn't it?

POETRY MEETS GRAPHIC DESIGN
Fuel, a design collective based in the United Kingdom, has become an independent publishing house as well as a service-based design agency. The edgy volume shown here pairs poet Ian McMillan with illustrator Andy Martin to create an unexpected book of poems. The result is a fresh and entertaining collision of art and language. Designed by Fuel.

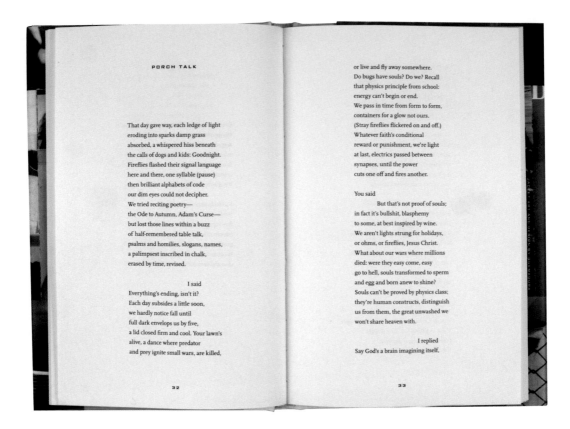

PORCH TALK

That day gave way, each ledge of light
eroding into sparks damp grass
absorbed, a whispered hiss beneath
the calls of dogs and kids: Goodnight.
Fireflies flashed their signal language
here and there, one syllable (pause)
then brilliant alphabets of code
our dim eyes could not decipher.
We tried reciting poetry—
the Ode to Autumn, Adam's Curse—
but lost those lines within a buzz
of half-remembered table talk,
psalms and homilies, slogans, names,
a palimpsest inscribed in chalk,
erased by time, revised.

              I said
Everything's ending, isn't it?
Each day subsides a little soon,
we hardly notice fall until
full dark envelops us by five,
a lid closed firm and cool. Your lawn's
alive, a dance where predator
and prey ignite small wars, are killed,

or live and fly away somewhere.
Do bugs have souls? Do we? Recall
that physics principle from school:
energy can't begin or end.
We pass in time from form to form,
containers for a glow not ours.
(Stray fireflies flickered on and off.)
Whatever faith's conditional
reward or punishment, we're light
at last, electrics passed between
synapses, until the power
cuts one off and fires another.

You said
          But that's not proof of souls;
in fact it's bullshit, blasphemy
to some, at best inspired by wine.
We aren't lights strung for holidays,
or ohms, or fireflies, Jesus Christ.
What about our wars where millions
died: were they easy come, easy
go to hell, souls transformed to sperm
and egg and born anew to shine?
Souls can't be proved by physics class;
they're human constructs, distinguish
us from them, the great unwashed we
won't share heaven with.

             I replied
Say God's a brain imagining itself.

32

33

INDEPENDENT PRESS

The Apparitioners, a volume of poems by George Witte, is published by Three Rail Press, an independent publisher based in Seattle, Washington. The design of this hardbound book reflects the standards of traditional book design with a subtle contemporary edge; note the geometric typeface used for poem title and page numbers. Jacket and book design by Quemadura.

"ich bin wegen der Veranstaltung hier" sagte der Mann
und suchte unter Franks Hemd nach der Eingangs-Tür

"ich bin kein Theater" sagte Frank

es kamen noch viele mehr
sie alle standen an

muss er sie alle einlassen?

viele unter ihren Schirmen

und eine Blinde
wartete
mit Hund

"es wird sagenhaft" sagte wer
"aber wann lässt er uns ein?"

Franks Tränen flossen
weil jemand riss seine Türen auf
und sie füllten ihn
eine Stunde lang

"I'm here for the show" the man said
looking under Frank's shirt for the door

"I'm no theater" Frank said

a line formed

must he admit them all?

many had umbrellas

a blind woman
waited with
her dog

"it's gonna be a great show" someone said
"but when's he gonna let us in?"

Frank's tears began to fall

someone ripped his doors open

they filled him for an hour

HARDCORE DIY

Poet Carrie Hunter is founder of
Ypolita Press. Her publications include
The Frank Poems by CA Conrad (in
English with a German translation).
This staple-bound, desktop-printed
chapbook takes a do-it-yourself
approach to publishing. The book is
available online via Hunter's blog,
ypolitapress.blogspot.com and at
selected bookstores. Cover art by
Cathleen Miller.

ZINES

by Ryan Clifford and Tony Venne

ZINES RUN THE GAMUT FROM STAPLE-BOUND BOOKLETS PRODUCED ON THE CHEAP AT THE LOCAL KINKO'S TO GLOSSY, FULL-COLOR PUBLICATIONS. Whatever the process, zines are produced by creative people with independent visions and commitments to looking at quirky content from their own points of view.

Zines have been a vital form of indie publishing for decades. Originating as cut-and-paste productions sent through the mail or sold at zine fairs, the contemporary zine is just as often produced via digital printing and marketed online. The attraction of this handy medium lies in its accessibility and ease of production as well as its relaxed, ephemeral character. Some zines speak to devoted subcultures, while others reach out to broader audiences. A homegrown zine can evolve into a bona fide periodical, with advertising, formal distribution, paid contributors, and a regular publication schedule. Other zines exist not to serve an audience but to satisfy the expressive impulses of their makers.

To produce your own zine, think about your skills, your passions, and your resources. The best zines come out of a deep interest in a subject area or a compelling desire to make and disseminate original art, poetry, writing, or photography. Many zines have a single creator, while others result from collaboration.

ZINE SCENE

Zines are fun to buy, trade, read, and collect. Most of all, zines are fun to make. Be your own editor, designer, photographer, art director, and publisher. Shown here are some of our favorite zines. On the top of the pile is a zine made in a weekend with Mike Perry and a team of graphic design MFA students at MICA (Maryland Institute College of Art).

The zine shown here was created during a weekend workshop led by designer and illustrator Mike Perry. He marshalled a team of sixteen designers who worked together to create a thirty-two-page zine in seventy-two hours. How do you find subject matter for a zine? This zine tackles an absurdly vast subject (science) from a humorous point of view. There was no time for research, so each contributor identified themes, from UFOs and the Big Bang to scientology and psychology, and endowed them with a graphic spin.

The team chose a large format (10.75 x 16 inches), creating a roomy playground for wide-open visual play. The saddle-stitched piece is offset printed in two colors of ink (pink and green), which mix to make brown. Working within this limited palette, everyone was free to create images, patterns, textures, type, and hand lettering. Drawings and letters were scanned as high-resolution bitmaps, which can be quickly changed into the designated ink colors via page design software. Layouts were passed around from designer to designer to keep the overall feeling loose and communal.

To help fund the publication, teammates called up their friends and family to fill up a page of funky classified-style ads at the back of the book.

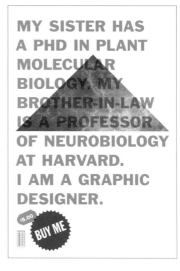

TEAM WORK
Sixteen designers spent a long weekend cranking out this zine about no small topic: science. Designed by Mike Perry and the Graphic Design MFA Studio at Maryland Institute College of Art (MICA).

BIG IDEAS

Everyone loosened up and tackled the grandiose subject matter from a pop-culture point of view. The result is a visual zine that showcases the team's combined visual sensibilities and collective sense of humor.

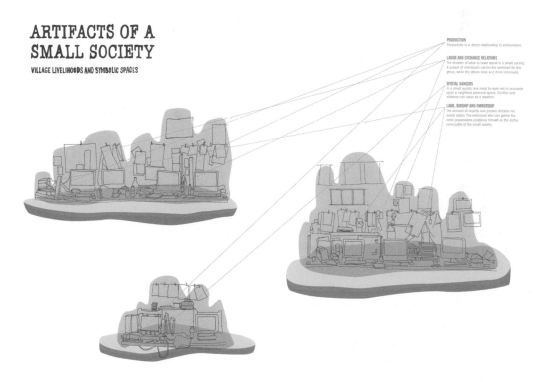

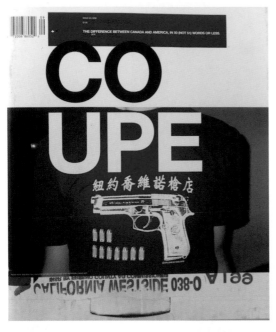

COUPE MAGAZINE

Coupe is a biannual publication produced by the design firm The Bang in Toronto. Each issue explores a single theme, often dealing with Canadian life and culture. Past issues have focused on the best typographic destinations in Toronto, the uniqueness of the Canadian experience, and Canada's relationship with border cities in the United States (including Detroit, Michigan, and Buffalo). *Coupe* is a showcase for graphic design, giving its producers a chance to experiment with the medium of publishing using their own content. This saddle-stitched zine employs full-color offset printing as well as special printing techniques such as thermography and varnish.

BLAM! BLAM!

This full-color offset printed publication is an erotic magazine for women. It was founded in 2006 by Jenna Leskela and Michelle Scifers, who wanted to create a publication where women could explore their sexuality without feeling exploited. *Blam! Blam!* features erotic fiction, original photography, and sensible how-to and advice writing.

The zine is purposefully small (5.5 x 8.5), allowing the reader to carry it around in a bag or read it in private. Photographic vignettes play a large part in the design of the layouts, which entice reader's imagination. The imagery is narrative rather than iconic. The typography is kept large to allow for low-light reading in bed. Throughout the magazine are several small ads that cater to the audience and help offset the costs of printing and distribution. *Blam! Blam!* is available online via subscription as well as at many independent and adult bookstores.

Issue I   Summer 2006

The Teacher
by Michelle Scifers

The morning sun peered through the blinds and I awoke. Instantly, I was hit with the aroma of my lover. A reminder that his beautiful nude body was in my presence. I rolled onto him and kissed his neck. I slowly began to caress his fair, soft skin.

At last, his eyes fluttered as he began to drift out of sleep. He grabbed my breast and my hand drifted towards his hard penis. I began to rub him and watched his face as he fully awakened. I had never given him a hand job at this point, it isn't my forte. I am not awful, mind you. I tend to shy away from things that I know I could do better. Right now, I didn't care. I wanted to please him. I wanted to please him and I wanted him to show me how I could. As he became more excited, I unleashed my secret. "I am not the best at these," I said. As if he read my mind, he asked

25

26

TICKLED PINK

Tickled Pink is an art zine produced by Todd Bratrud. It features illustrations influenced by pop culture and the skateboarding underground.

The design is reminiscent of an old-school single-color zine, but in addition to black, other spot colors are used to strong effect. Direct, clear line work balances detailed drawings that depict recognizable pop culture icons as well as other characters that are not as recognizable, drawn from the artist's imagination.

Tickled Pink is printed on pink paper stock and packaged with several stickers and other elements. (The issue shown here comes with a piece of X-ray film.) The zine is produced in editions of one hundred and is available from a few specialty book sellers, including Burlesque of North America.

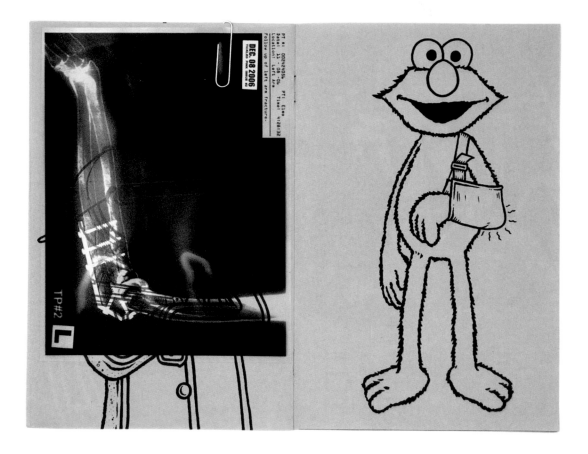

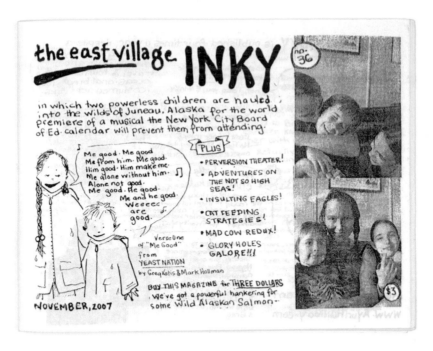

EAST VILLAGE INKY

The *East Village Inky* was begun by Ayun Halliday in 1993 on her daughter's first birthday. This simple zine centers around Ayun's experience as a mother in New York City. It chronicles her day-to-day errand running, traveling, and activities with her two children, Inky and Milo. Each issue contains stories, comics, and recipes as well as drawings and photographs of the kids. This photocopied zine has an economical format (5.5 x 4.25 inches), bound with a single staple. It's filled from edge-to-edge with handwritten texts and simple drawings. The images are integrated with the writing, giving the issues a cohesive look and a handmade feel. The *East Village Inky* is available at several independent bookstores and children's shops throughout the country. Halliday also distributes it on her website, along with other publications she has produced.

PICTURE BOOKS FOR KIDS

by April Osmanof

EVERYBODY AND THEIR MOTHER WANTS TO WRITE A CHILDREN'S BOOK. Yet the market for juvenile literature is fiercely competitive, making it tough for new authors and illustrators to break in. If once upon a time you had a brilliant idea for a picture book for kids, now could be the time to publish it yourself.

Many an indie children's book is inspired by the author's own little relatives—kids and grandkids, nieces and nephews. Perhaps your book is the perfect gift for a child in your life (and for other kids, too).

The book showcased here was produced using Lulu's print-on-demand service, which allows authors to share their books with friends, relatives, and a wider potential audience. Books can be produced in color with no start-up cost, and you can order as many prototypes as you want along the way.

Plan your book with real kids in mind. What age is your audience? How much text should fall on each page? Will your book be read aloud by an adult or directly by a child? How long does the book take to read? Spend time looking at successful children's literature and books you know and love. Study different styles of writing, illustration, and page layout. Amateurs' kids books often have a single picture on every page, with a blob of text underneath; flat and boring, such books lack variation in scale and layout from page to page. In a well-crafted picture book, images flow from one spread to the next, like scenes in a movie, with interesting cuts and transitions.

WHAT DO YOU LOOK LIKE WHEN ONLY YOUR BONES ARE SHOWING? This self-published book is directed at kids age four to seven. The illustrations are made with handcut adhesive contact paper. Written, designed, and illustrated by April Osmanof.

SKETCHING IDEAS

Make plenty of sketches based on your initial concept. *What Do You Look Like When Only Your Bones Are Showing?* is a book about accepting people's differences; we're all more or less the same on the inside. A short verse introduces each character, followed by an "X-ray" image of their bones.

Over here is a basketball player.
He's the tallest we've seen.
He might be too big
to fit in the machine.

EXECUTING IDEAS

Plain pencil sketches aren't exciting enough for a kid's book. These illustrations are collages made from sticky-backed contact paper. This fun technique allowed the illustrator to change and rearrange the hand-cut pieces before scanning them.

Let's look at a pirate
next to the sea.
His loot is buried there
right by that tree.

PAGE FORMATS

The kids' book shown here has square pages, a format that offers flexibility for placing words and images. Avoid making your pages 8.5 x 11. Many an editor's slush pile is stacked high with prototypes for kids' books printed out on standard letter paper, one picture per page. If you do work in 8.5 x 11, try binding your pages horizontally for a more surprising effect.

DISCOVER VARIETY

To make your book more cinematic, play with extreme close-ups as well as zooming out to show a larger scene or landscape. Use white space to give your readers a chance to breathe.

Here are some actors
who can sing and dance.
They took a break from
their play to give us
a glance.

WATCH THE SPINE

When your images cover full spreads or extend past a single page, don't put important visual information dead center. You don't want your main character's head to get chopped up in the binding.

CREATE CONSTANTS

In the book shown here, a common horizon line runs throughout all of the pages. You might want to keep your main character around the same size on each page or have the movement on each page follow in one direction.

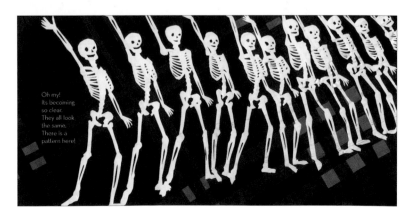

Oh my!
Its becoming
so clear.
They all look
the same.
There is a
pattern here!

DESMOND AND HIS MONSTER FRIENDS
The hand-lettered text works well with the
spunky illustrations. This self-published book
was printed on demand by Lulu. Design, text,
and illustrations by Sarah A. Mires; senior
thesis, Illustration Department, MICA.

A WHIRL IN A PEARL
This self-published book was produced in a small edition via print-on-demand. The author packaged it in a custom-made envelope to make the piece more personal. Written, designed, and illustrated by Erin Womack, The Lab, MICA.

CECIL'S NEW YEAR'S EVE TAIL
Buttonweed Press, located in Northfield, Minnesota, is a small producer of children's books dedicated to promoting acceptance of difference and identity. Story and pictures by Marie Fritz Perry.

PICTURE BOOKS FOR ADULTS

by Yue Tuo

PICTURE BOOKS AREN'T JUST FOR KIDS. Graphic novels and illustrated books have become important literary and artistic genres. Many artists enjoy putting their drawings into book form using a variety of techniques. Employ dynamic page design to bring napkin doodles and subway sketches to life. A book of drawings makes a wonderful gift, portfolio piece, or a work of art in its own right.

The books showcased in this chapter use images as dynamic pictorial matter. Unlike a book of reproductions, such as an exhibition catalog or scholarly art book, these works use images to tell a visual story. Pictures leap and wander off the page —like images in an illustrated book for kids. Books like these can be made by hand as one-of-a-kind art objects or printed in large or small editions.

Go through your old sketchbooks and rediscover the works of art you have made—beautiful or funny, raw or polished—and create a unique and personal publication.

SKETCHBOOK
This fun visual book consists of casual sketches that have been scanned, placed, and printed in a handmade volume. By changing the scale of images and laying them out in a dynamic way, the designer has given her sketches a new life. Illustrations and design by Yue Tuo.

TELLING A STORY

The book shown here is a collection of comic illustrations about everyday life in China. The pages are folded at the outer edge, or "fore edge," and they are sewn together with a stab binding. (Learn about this technique in our "Make Your Own Books" chapter.) The layout helps convey the playful mood of the book and suggests connections between pictures. Above, an old married couple who have gone to heaven are drawn standing on a pair of clouds. Another cloud floats off the top of the page.

It is fun to experiment with how images sit on the page and how they run off the edges or change orientation. Designed by Yue Tuo.

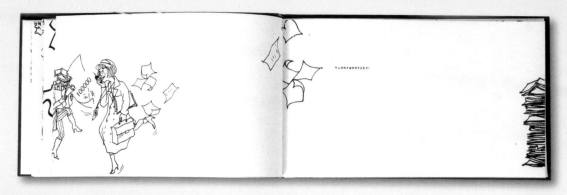

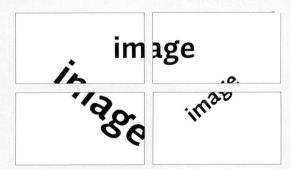

CUTTING AND REPEATING

A drawing can start on one page and continue on the next. Because the pages in this book are folded along the outside edge, the drawings can literally wrap from page to page. You can create a similar effect with normal pages printed back-to-back (although the images might not line up exactly, owing to the printing process). This layout technique creates a sense of continuity and movement in the book. Putting a small part of an image in the corner of the book tells the reader to turn the page.

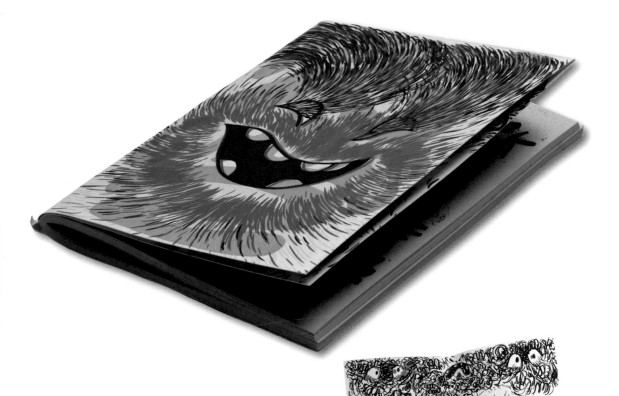

TOADS N CHODES

This staple-bound, photocopied book is transformed into a spectacular interactive object by a unique cover that folds out into a poster. The cover is screen-printed in multiple colors and employs large-scale imagery. For extra zip, the inside pages are printed on bright green stock. Designed by Noel Freibert, Extreme Troglodyte Press. Photos by Dan Meyers.

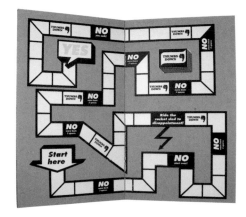

*MASSIVE GRAPHIC
This huge book of drawings and designs measures 11 x 18 inches. Screen printed on heavy board, the pages are perfect bound and edged with gold foil. Designed by Joseph Galbreath.

PICNIC AT TOUGH BEACH

This handmade comic book has a photocopied interior and a screen-printed cover. The cover is printed on both the inside and the outside, creating the effect of beautiful "endpapers" when you open the book. Interior pages are photocopied on pale coffee-colored stock. Designed by Ryan Smith. Photos by Dan Meyers.

CONVERSATIONS IN YOUR NEIGHBORHOOD

This book consists of a single piece of paper screen printed on both sides and folded down into a tiny volume. The novelty-style package emphasizes the book's toylike spirit. Designed by Ryan Smith. Photos by Dan Meyers.

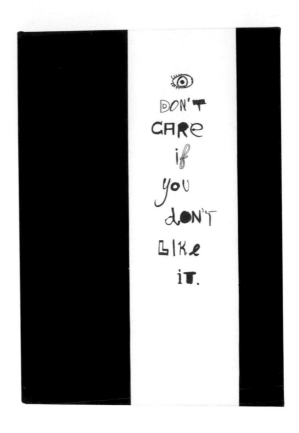

I DON'T CARE
IF YOU DON'T LIKE IT

This book consists of original sketches that were cut down and bound into a book. The sketches were created by students in a workshop led by designer and illustrator Laurie Rosenwald. The book was produced in an edition of five, and each one is unique. Designed by Joseph Galbreath.

TASTE
This photocopied journal pairs portraits of chairs with hand-lettered quotes about how people feel about their furniture. Designed by Tony Venne.

STRIP(E)
Banning S.P.
1995

EXHIBITION CATALOGS

by John Corrigan

WHEN ARTISTS OR CURATORS PRODUCE EXHIBITIONS, THEY PUT A LOT OF THOUGHT INTO HOW TO DISPLAY THE WORKS ON VIEW. How high should the pieces be hung, and in what order? Are the works framed or unframed, close together or spread far apart? Are the pieces in dialog with each other, or is each one a self-contained statement? Will the work be identified with labels on the wall or with a printed list? Similar design decisions go into making an exhibition catalog or any book of photographs and reproductions of works of art.

Such books present and display reproductions in a manner that makes the works compelling and accessible to readers. An art or photography book is a document of works that exist elsewhere. Often, the photographs in a book are the only permanent record of an installation or performance. The printed page is no substitute for experiencing art in the flesh, even though the quality and availability of color reproductions has increased rapidly over the past decade. Just as a documentary film is an edited, authored depiction of reality, so an exhibition catalog or other art book is an edited, staged selection of images. The seemingly neutral, anonymous format of many art books has been deliberately designed in order to create an authoritative yet inviting atmosphere for looking at reproductions. Layout and typography emphasize the work, while the book itself steps into the background.

ON DISPLAY

Like a well-designed gallery show, a thoughtfully produced catalog or art book aims to highlight the art, showing it off to its best advantage. Simple layouts with generous white space and elegant captions will help make the artwork look good. Design and photography by John Corrigan.

An art book is an invaluable tool for artists who want to document their work and share it with various audiences, including collectors, curators, collaborators, grants organizations, fellow artists, and the general public. Creating a clean, simple design that focuses attention on the work is a good place to start. Use scale, rhythm, sequence, and white space to present a selection of images in an inviting manner.

Arrange works in a sequence that encourages dialogue and comparison between images. At the same time, understand that readers will be free to flip through your book and stop where their interest takes them. A good art book or exhibition catalog creates opportunities to wander and rest—just like a good exhibition design.

Pictures are often the dominant content of an exhibition catalog, although you may also want to include essays, captions, and a checklist. An essay by a critic or writer adds weight and value to your book. Commissioning an original text is a great way to collaborate with a writer and acquire fresh insight about an artist's work. A checklist is a complete list of all the works that were featured in the exhibition, including those that may not appear in the catalog. This document, which typically includes titles of works, dimensions, media, and other basic information, becomes an official record of the exhibition's content, valuable to curators, researchers, artists, and dealers.

STUDY YOUR PICTURES
Look at all your pictures before choosing what shape your book will be. If most of your pictures are horizontal, for example, you may prefer a horizontal book. Also consider the length and importance of your captions. These take up more room on the page than you might expect.

VERTICAL FORMAT (RIGHT)
Vertical pages are the most familiar to readers. This format works well for showing one image per page with a caption underneath. You might also put all your images on the right page and captions on the left page.

LANDSCAPE FORMAT (BELOW)
The extra page width in a horizontal publication easily accommodates multiple images, explanatory text, and captions. Try leaving white space around an image to emphasize its object-like quality.

CHOOSING A FORMAT
Your choice of format will be influenced by the printing method you choose to use as well as by your book's content. Some page sizes are more economical than others, and some printers only produce books in certain sizes. The horizontal format chosen for this book relates to the experience of walking through a gallery. The wide format also makes it easy to place two square or vertical images on a single page, while leaving plenty of room for captions. Designed by John Corrigan.

FOREWORD

All of the images in this exhibition were created using a Polaroid Land Camera. The photographs have been left unaltered, full framed and reflect a single moment. Using the immediacy of the Polaroid one knows whether the image is to be kept, or destroyed.

Central Air: Nomadic Art Space began in 1999. Initially started as Radiator Art Exhibition Company, with co-founder Lee Anne Swanson, its mission was to create a collective art space allowing founding members to exhibit and promote their work as well as the works of like minded artists. Radiator radically provided an exhibition space for group shows as well as thematic artist pairings. Radiator looked to reinvigorate the exhibition options in Minneapolis.

Central Air was the next generation. I wanted to curate a scene or happening. I wanted to publish the involvement of multiple disciplined contributor's. The nomadic essence of an art exhibition represents itself perfectly in a publication, avoiding the gallery atmosphere altogether.

The context for *No Negative* came from the realization that these Polaroid images, taken by Jerome Paige Tobias from 1992-1997, remain the only documentation of his experience with these seemingly obscure places. Jerome is repeatedly drawn to architectural anomalies, as well as his interaction with and memory of these places. These photographs identify obscure landmarks without direct reference. Yet Jerome can actively identify the moment and placement of each photograph.

This collection celebrates the chosen limitations of using a Polaroid Land Camera. The photographer medium of the Polaroid, unlike any other camera, relies on the moment of observation. The final image implies the informal documentation of fleeting time. Polaroid images appear small, frail, and delicate in comparison to other photographic formats. The moments between the click of the shutter and the peeling of the emulsion paper consist of hope and anticipation, this represents itself in the final presentation of the image.

The images of this photographic exhibition are snap shots of specific places at specific moments. The photographs are grouped according to repeated interest, and represent the collected memories of both place and space.

4 \\ CENTRAL AIR NOMADIC ART SPACE

NO NEGATIVE \\ 5

DOCUMENTED
PLACE

FREE HBO
Minneapolis, Minnesota
1995

DESIGNING A GRID

A grid consists of the columns and margins of your book as well as horizontal divisions. Designers use grids to create consistent yet varied pages, making their publications feel orderly and professional. They allow the designer to create many different layouts—you don't have to stick everything in the middle of the page. To make a grid, begin by choosing how many columns your pages will have. Page layout programs such as InDesign will ask you to create columns when you open a new document. The grid shown here has five columns per page. Some elements, like captions, occupy just one column, while pictures and essays span multiple columns. This grid has five horizontal divisions as well as five vertical columns. The grid serves to anchor different types of information, such as headlines, captions, running heads, and page numbers (also called folios). The grid creates order while allowing elements to be placed in a dynamic, changing pattern.

IMAGE SIZE AND PLACEMENT

Each double-page spread of your book is a unit. Think about the relationship between the images on the left and right pages. Should each image be large or small? Do you need to show a detail of an image? Use the grid to determine both the size and position of images. Ignore the grid when you feel it's necessary.

Also think about how big to make your images. Some artists want to make each picture as large as possible on the page. Others want to suggest the scale of the actual art works by making some reproductions smaller than others. You may wish to create scales that are unrelated to the artwork's actual size. For example, you could

come in close on a tiny painting and show off its details, or your could zoom out to represent a sculptural object in a larger environment.

OTHER HEROES

This catalog for an exhibition about African-American comic artists was produced via Lulu's print-on-demand service. Curators John Jennings and Damian Duffy had a tiny budget but wanted to document and disseminate their research in a more permanent way. Designed by John Jennings. Photos by Jason Okutake.

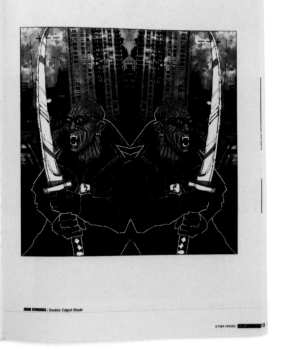

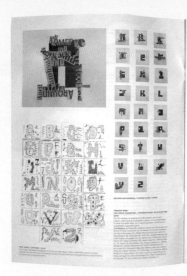

ALPHABET

Nolen Strals and Bruce Willen of Post Typography created this book to document their traveling exhibition Alphabet. The book and exhibition feature sixty-three alphabets drawn by fifty-one artists and designers from around the world. Strals and Willen wanted to "remove each alphabet from the context of words and typography" so that viewers would focus on the twenty-six shapes of each featured alphabet. The book is offset printed in black and white and saddle stitched.

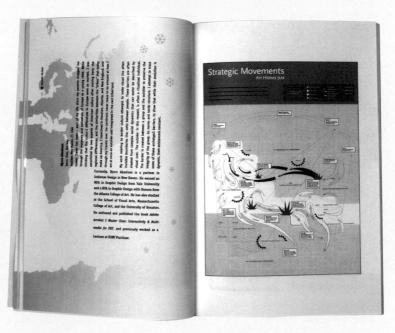

OUTSIDE IN

In 2005 twenty-five designers from all over the world decided to put together a book of posters. All of the designers consider themselves "outsiders" in one way or another (immigrants, nomads, refugees, etc.). The posters in the book illustrate these designers' feelings of displacement. Outside In was organized into a book format by Maya Drozdz, who runs the design studio VisuaLingual in Cincinnati, Ohio. The book is produced via print-on-demand by Lulu, which can reach audiences in numerous countries worldwide.

PORTFOLIOS

by HyunSoo Lim

TIME WAS WHEN THE WORD "PORTFOLIO" CONJURED AN IMAGE OF A HUGE FAUX LEATHER CASE WITH A ZIPPER ALONG THE OUTSIDE AND DUSTY PLASTIC SLEEVES FILLED WITH GLUE-STAINED PROJECTS. Today, a portfolio is more likely to be a compact printed book produced in multiples. Relatively inexpensive to produce, you can mail a printed book to potential clients or galleries, include it with applications for grants and fellowships, or leave it behind at a job interview.

The portfolio shown here was made for Hwa Youn Lee, an illustrator. Although she also has a portfolio of original drawings and tear sheets from client projects, she has found many advantages to having a printed piece like this one as well. This book of her work also helps art directors and clients imagine Lee's drawings in print. Presented in her portfolio are many works with different themes, materials and sizes. Laid out on the pages of a book, they clearly represent the style and vision of a single artist.

The portfolio was produced using Lulu's print-on-demand service. Lee can order just a few copies at a time, and it is easy to update the pages with new work and order more copies as needed. You could also make an artist's portfolio using a desktop printer and bind it using one of the methods described in the "Make Your Own Books" section of this guide.

SHOW YOURSELF OFF

A print-on-demand portfolio is a convenient way to share your work with potential clients. Use layout to tell a story and dramatize details. Illustrations by Hwa Youn Lee. Design by HyunSoo Lim.

LAYING OUT THE OPENING PAGES OF A PORTFOLIO Shown here are pages from a portfolio created for illustrator Hwa Youn Lee. One of her drawings is very long and skinny: over 32 inches long and only 2.1 inches tall. Designer HyunSoo Lim used this unusual image as an opportunity to create an exciting series of opening pages. The drawing starts on the first page and runs over the next two spreads. The portfolio was printed and bound via print-on-demand and can be easily updated.

Do you want to see my dreams?

Portfolio

Works by Hwa Youn Lee

Kitting Monster
Ink and pen on paper, 2.1 X 32.7 in.

My Heavy Balloon,
Mixed media, 6.5 X 9.9 in.

Everybody, I Am Meditating,
Mixed media, 6.5 X 9.9 in.

Dream to Fly,
Mixed media, 6.5 X 9.9 in.

Right: Under My Bed Quilt,
Mixed media, 6.5 X 9.9 in.

For My Gift,
Mixed media, 6.5 X 9.9 in.

I'm Tired,
Mixed media, 6.5 X 9.9 in.

Above: An Elevator,
Mixed media, 6.5 X 9.9 in.

RHYTHM AND SCALE

Use changes in scale to create variety and make a conversation among the pictures. Presenting the works at different sizes makes the pages dynamic. Borders, white space, and background color help to frame each work.

ROXANA ZARGHAM

Graphic designer Roxana Zargham has treated her portfolio
as a visual tour de force. Rather than neatly document her
projects individually, she allows them to overlap and
overprint in rich layers. The pages are unbound, giving each
one the feeling of a work of art. Photos by Dan Meyers.

MARC BURCKHARDT

Artist Marc Burckhardt sends out a small, beautifully produced volume of his work during the winter holidays. Although the booklets are saddle stitched, Burckhardt uses a gatefolded jacket with foil-stamped cover imagery in addition to high-quality paper and printing to make each one a special keepsake.

REBECA MÉNDEZ

DESIGNER & ARTIST LIVING IN LOS ANGELES

SHORT CV

SELECTED BIBLIOGRAPHY

09.2007

REBECA MÉNDEZ

Graphic designer and artist Rebeca Méndez creates these booklets to document each of her projects. The pages are laser printed and sewn together using the pamphlet-stitch method. (Learn how in our "Make Your Own Books" chapter.) As a faculty member in the art and design program at UCLA, Méndez requires her students to document their projects in all her courses. These simple but elegant publications become a permanent record of ongoing work. Photos by Dan Meyers.

STEVEN AND WILLIAM LADD

This deluxe, hand-bound portfolio documents the work of
Steven and William Ladd, two designers of jewelry and
fashion accessories with a studio in New York City. The book
documents their sketches and work process as well as their
finished pieces. It is as impeccably crafted as their jewelry
and other objects. Photos by Dan Meyers.

MAKE YOUR OWN BOOKS

Production Basics—Handmade Books

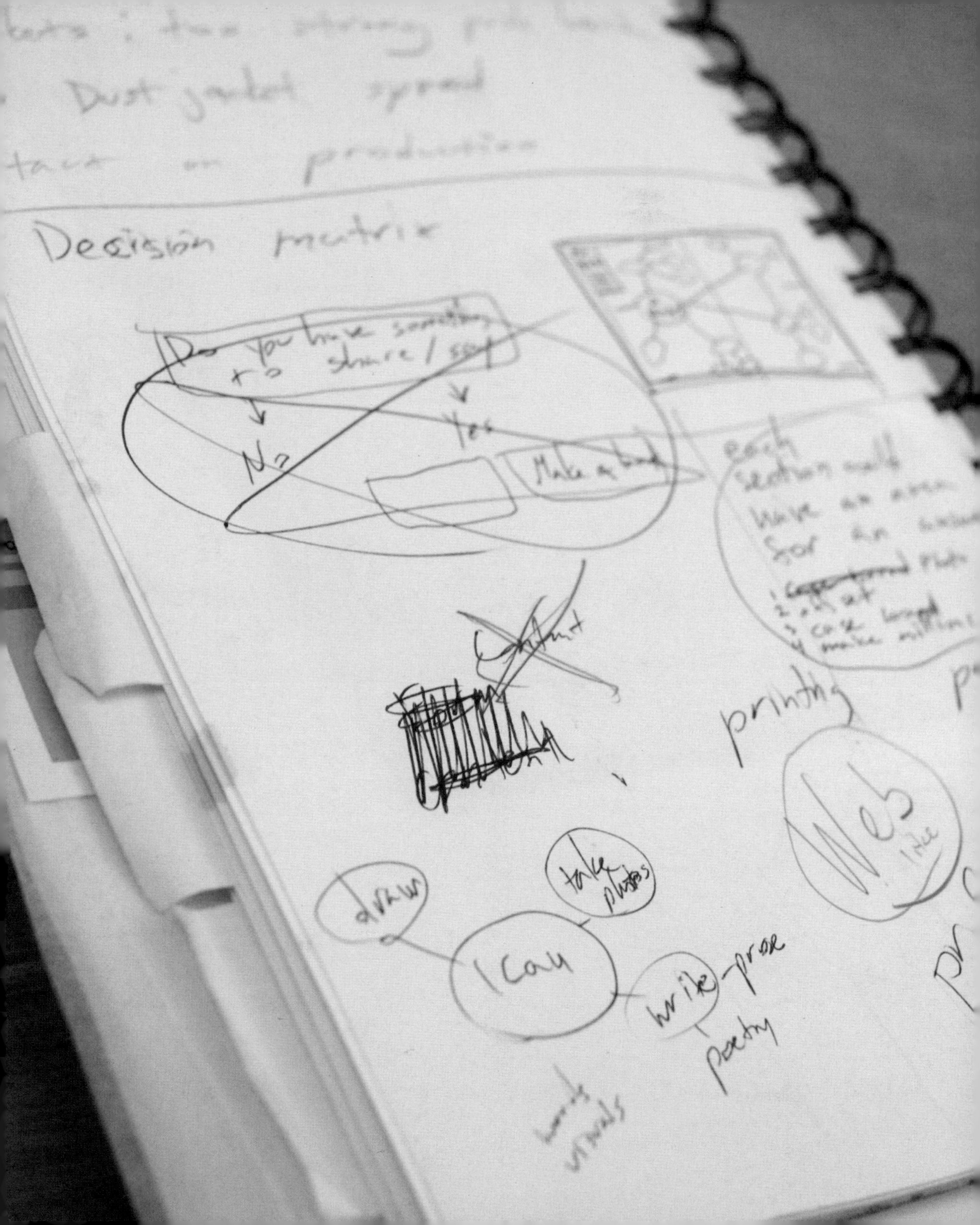

Dust jacket spread

tate on production

Decision matrix

Do you have something to share / say?

No → Yes → Make a book

each section will have an area for an

printing

Web

draw

take photos

I can

write prose poetry

PRODUCTION BASICS

by Joseph Galbreath

THERE ARE THREE BASIC WAYS TO PRODUCE YOUR BOOK: HARDCORE DIY, PRINT ON DEMAND, AND CONVENTIONAL PRINTING. The design guidelines that we explored in the previous section are relevant to all of these production methods, which range from down-and-dirty techniques that you can pull off with equipment in your own home, school, or office to the high-end approach pursued by professional publishers.

Making books by hand is an art and craft of the highest order. It's also an industrial process that is considered the oldest form of mass-production. This chapter explains some basic bookmaking techniques as well as how to work with manufacturers who can produce larger quantities on your behalf. The design of your book is interdependent with how it will be physically produced. How big will your pages be, and how many will you have? How will the book be bound? How many copies will you need? All these decisions will affect the look and feel of your book, as well as the cost of producing it. Follow our flow chart on the following spread to figure out the best (or worst) ways to plunge into the strange and exciting world of self-publishing.

MAKE A PLAN

Whether you are making your book by hand or working with a commercial printing service, you will need a plan of action. Know your schedule, your budget, and your skills. What can you do yourself? Where will you need help? Drawing and photograph by Joseph Galbreath.

HOW WILL YOU PRODUCE YOUR BOOK?

HANDS FREE

BY HAND

What is your budget?

| BUDGET? | BUDGET! |

Print on Demand

Conventional

Which POD service will you use?

_____
NAME OF SERVICE PROVIDER

| NOT SURE |

Who will print your book?

_____
NAME OF PRINTER

| NOT SURE |

Research printers and request quotes.

Select all that apply:

☐ 4.25 x 6.875 in   ☐ Color
☐ 5.25 x 8   ☐ Black/white
☐ 6 x 9   ☐ Coil bound
☐ 6.14 x 9.21   ☐ Saddle stitch
☐ 6.5 x 9   ☐ Perfect bound
☐ 7 x 10   ☐ Dust jacket
☐ 7.44 x 9.68   ☐ Case wrap
☐ 7.5 x 7.5
☐ 8.25 x 8.25
☐ 8.25 x 6   **Research which**
☐ 8.27 x 11.69   **service best**
☐ 8.5 x 8.5   **meets these**
☐ 9 x 7   **requirements.**

Will you attend press checks and bindery OKs?

| YES | NO |

Who will distribute your book?

| NOT SURE |

_____
NAME OF DISTRIBUTOR

List five people who will store twenty boxes of books for an indefinite amount of time:

1 _____
2 _____
3 _____
4 _____
5 _____

_____
NAME OF SERVICE PROVIDER

Very few people make serious money publishing books. Even well-known authors are advised to keep their day jobs. Do a profit-and-loss analysis and decide how much you're willing to spend and how many copies you'd have to sell to break even.

Have you made books by hand before?

YES **NO**

Will you be trying any new techniques?

NO **YES**

Do you have all the supplies you need?

YES **NOT SURE**

Consult tutorials and look for a list of required tools.

Go shopping.

How many books will you make?

QTY _____ **NOT SURE**

How much time will it take to build each book?

_____ HRS **X2**

Consult your budget.

How many relatives, friends, and coworkers do you have?

What would you do with extra books?

Do you plan on selling your book?

YES **NO**

Where?

What is your budget?

$ _____ **NOT SURE**

How will you print your book?

☐ Photocopy **LEAST EXPENSIVE**
☐ Ink jet
☐ Color laser
☐ Letterpress
☐ Screen print
☐ Offset lithography **MOST EXPENSIVE**
☐ Other

How will you bind your book?

☐ Stapled **LEAST TIME/SUPPLIES**
☐ Screw post
☐ Sewn
☐ Perfect **MOST TIME/SUPPLIES**
☐ Other

List and contact five places that might be interested in selling your book:

1 _____
2 _____
3 _____
4 _____
5 _____

ANY TAKERS?

NO **YES**

CONGRATULATIONS! You are a self-published author.

Still have something to say?

YES **NO**

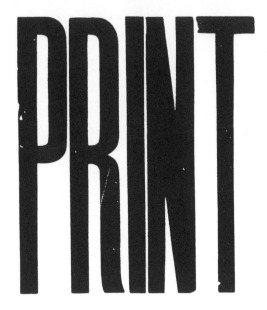

LETTERPRESS

Above is a printed sample of the wood type block that appears on the opposite page. Traditional letterpress printing uses individual characters cast from lead or carved from wood. Large-scale letters are usually made from wood, which is lighter than lead. But even wood wears out over time. Marks and nicks create an unexpected and imperfect surface that gives letterpress its unusual charm.

Types of Printing

Although budget, quantity, and content are considerations in any publishing venture, deciding how to print an indie book will also be influenced by your personal skill set, access to materials and equipment, and how much time you wish to invest. (Remember that however much time you think the project will take, you should double it to be safe.)

If your downstairs neighbor runs a letterpress shop, do stop by and introduce yourself. If you live in the remote hills of Montana, learn what you can achieve working over the internet. If you're in orange-alert rush mode, crank out your stapled zine at Kinko's. If you've got time to spend on proofing and refinements, produce your 300-page novel via print-on-demand. Take a look at the broad range of processes available and the advantages and limitations of each one before choosing what's best for your project. Each technology is intriguing—and annoying—in its own way.

PHOTOCOPY

Informal and immediate, this is one of the fastest and cheapest ways to get text and image on paper for short-run projects. All you need is source material and a photocopier. For interest, use colored paper or found paper. For editions bigger than a few hundred, explore offset or digital printing as cheaper options.

INK JET / COLOR LASER

Design a book on your computer and hit the print button. Desktop printers use process colors—cyan, magenta, yellow, and black—that allow for full-color imagery. Larger format printers are available (for a higher cost, of course, and more real estate on your proverbial desktop). Some ink jet printers use archival inks. Be aware that some printing paper is coated and will not fold nicely, so experiment before choosing the best stock for your book. Desktop printing is not cost effective for large editions, but it is an easy entry point for producing some-of-a-kind books.

LETTERPRESS

Once the standard for commercial printing, letterpress is now primarily a cottage industry. A raised surface is inked and pressed onto the page, resulting in rich, tactile prints. Letterpress purists prefer working with metal and wood type (individual relief letter blocks that are assembled by hand), but digital files can be turned into film and burned onto polymer plates. Although letterpress printing has become popular for invitations and fine press projects, letterpress shops are not available in every area, and this is an expensive technology for multipage projects. It is excellent for printing fine details and small text.

SCREEN PRINT

Also known as serigraphy or silk screen printing, this method forces ink through a stenciled mesh screen with a squeegee onto a variety of substrates, including paper, fabric, glass, plastic, and metal. Tiny text and detailed pictures will not hold up well, so this technique is not generally used for text-heavy books with fussy illustrations. While most professional shops use mechanical equipment, a wide range of amateur set-ups can be assembled with readily available tools and supplies—making screen printing an indie favorite. This technique is labor intensive but lets you physically participate in the printing process.

DIGITAL OR PRINT-ON-DEMAND

Because digital files are interpreted electronically directly on the drums of the press, numerous pages can be printed quickly with minimal prep time, making short-run jobs economically feasible. Digital printing is toner based, not ink based, so flaking can occur around folds. Less expensive than offset printing, quality varies, so request printed samples. Be sure to review a proof of your project before proceeding with the whole job to ensure that the color and overall quality meets your expectations.

OFFSET LITHOGRAPHY

This is the standard printing method for most commercially printed material. Plates are made for each ink and offset onto rollers which then transfer the ink to the paper. Offset is known for its consistent print quality. It is ideal for large quantities; while there is substantial cost in preparing the printing plates, printing more copies spreads out that cost. Most cities of modest size have several printing companies to choose from. It is common practice to review proofs before the plates are made and to attend press checks and okay the final press run.

Types of binding

There are many ways to fasten loose pages together to form a book. Binding agents include adhesive, staples, and thread; more complex bindings may employ several materials. Much like selecting a printing process, the decision of how to bind your indie book will be influenced by cost, practicality, and durability. How thick is your book? Should it lie flat? How will the binding affect the cost per unit?

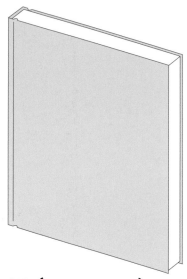

CASE (AKA HARDCOVER)

The pages form signatures that are sewn using thread and then glued to linen tape for flexibility and strength. The block of signatures (text block) is trimmed and fastened to the case (front cover, spine, and back cover) with endpapers. Case-bound books lie flat and are extremely durable.

PERFECT

Loose pages are adhered with glue along their bound edge. The cover is then wrapped around and glued. Small quantities can be produced by hand if you have access to a guillotine cutter or are working with machine-cut leafs of paper. Perfect-bound books do not lie flat.

TAPE

A cloth tape treated with heat-sensitive glue is wrapped around the assembled covers and pages. Heat is applied, causing the glue to adhere to the pages and cover. Tape-bound books lie flat.

SIDE STITCH

Pages and covers are stapled through from front to the back. Because the binding runs through the edge of the book, small volumes will loose a great deal of visual real estate in the gutter. The thickness of the book determines the practicality of this binding method. Side-stitched books do not lie flat.

SADDLE STITCH

Cover and pages are folded and stapled. Because the entire book is folded in half, there is a maximum thickness of about a half inch for effective saddle stitching. Saddle-stitched books lie flat and can be inexpensively produced either by machine or with a long-necked stapler.

PAMPHLET STITCH

This technique is similar to saddle stitch. The cover and pages are sewn together with thread and then tied off. The knot and ends remain visible. This hand process is usually used for small quantities of publications with thirty-six pages or fewer. Pamphlets lie flat.

SCREW AND POST

Covers and pages are drilled and bound with a threaded post and screw. The cover then turns back on itself to hide the fastening. Pages can easily be added or subtracted. Books must be hand assembled. Post-bound books do not lie flat.

STAB

Stab is also referred to as Japanese stab binding. Sheets are sewn together such that the thread is visible on the spine and sides of the book. This binding creates a large gutter that should be accounted for while designing. Stab-bound books do not lie flat.

SPIRAL

Holes are punched through the pages with a machine, and then a wire coil is spun up the spine of the book. Spiral-bound books lie flat.

PLASTIC COMB

This is the most hideous binding method of all and should never be used. The plastic comb is ugly, and the bound books do not lie flat.

Working with Commercial Printing Services

If you decide not to print your book yourself using your desktop printer or other DIY technologies (potato printing? rubber stamps?), you will have to work with a commercial printer. Here is an overview of some of the available services.

Print-on-Demand (POD) services are useful if you can't afford the cost of printing many books at once. Various companies work with authors and publishers to print and bind a book only when a customer orders it. The unit cost will be much higher than that of a mass-produced book, but you won't need much capital to start. Indeed, some services offer their basic services for free. (You pay only when you order copies, and there is no minimum order.)

Be warned that you are unlikely to ever make a big profit with POD publishing, because the economy of scale is working against you. The unit cost of a POD book is usually too high to make it a viable product for bookstore distribution, because both the distributor and the bookstore need to add a

Publishing Services

LULU has a user-friendly interface and a wide range of formats, and it's free. There is no minimum order, and the print quality is decent. Basic design skills required: you will need to design and edit your book yourself and upload it as a PDF.

FEDEX/KINKO'S and other copy centers have evolved into substantial POD providers. Visit your local store and take a look at all the while-you-wait printing and binding options. Saddle stitch and glue binding are especially useful.

BLURB provides users with its own free book design software, so you don't need to have a page layout program or any substantial technical skills. The resulting designs are attractive in a somewhat sterile, standardized way. (If you want more control over your layouts and typography, you can upload JPEGs instead of using Blurb's layout software.)

BOOKSURGE is an Amazon subsidiary that specializes in POD. BookSurge has services for both authors and publishers. It charges a fee to create a user's account and begin the process. The fee includes an ISBN that will be owned by BookSurge. You can also provide your own ISBN. All BookSurge books are offered for sale on Amazon.

SELF-PUBLISHING COMPANIES charge authors a fee for services including design, editing, printing, and distribution. In some cases, the subsidy publisher owns the rights to the finished book (but not to its content), and it issues the book under its own publishing name. In other instances, the company only produces the book; the author is the work's official publisher and owns all rights. Read all agreements carefully to find an appropriate service, and always take a look at sample publications. Self-publishing services can be found easily via internet search; a few include iUniverse, AuthorHouse, and Dog Ear Publishing.

substantial sum on top of the basic unit cost. (See more below about distributing your book.) But if you are looking to make a small number of books for a focused audience, POD is a great system that is becoming hipper and more widely used as new companies enter the marketplace.

Conventional Printing requires you to produce a substantial quantity of books in advance (1,000 copies or more). Your cost will vary depending on the size, binding method, number of pages, use of color, type of paper, number of pictures, and other factors, but whatever your specifications are, you will need to outlay some significant cash upfront. The more copies you print, the lower the unit cost for each book (and the greater your initial investment). This principle is called "economy of scale," and it is the core idea behind all mass production.

Commercial offset printers exist in every urban area; a designer will typically request estimates from several printers, based on a detailed description of the project. You can find a printer through word of mouth, talking to other artists, designers, or authors, or you can go online or open the phone book. You might also choose to work with a print broker who has relationships with many different printing companies, including factories in Asia and other parts of the world. If you intend to make a serious profit on your book in the long term, conventional printing is the way to go.

Requesting an Estimate

If you are working with a commercial printer, provide the following specifications when requesting an estimate:

QUANTITY You can ask for pricing on a range of quantities—1,000/2,000/5,000, for example. The cost per unit will decrease as the number of units increases.

TIMING Do you need the books for an exhibition opening next week? Be realistic; printing is a physical process that takes time to prepare and implement.

TRIM SIZE What are the outside measurements of the page? Some sizes will be more economical than others, depending on your printer's press size and paper stock.

PAGE COUNT How many pages will the book have? If your book is made from folded pages (as in a saddle stitched or sewn book), the page count must be in multiples of four. Multiples of sixteen are most common for substantial publications. A glued or spiral-bound book is bound in multiples of two.

NUMBER OF COLORS Full color photography is printed in four process colors: cyan, magenta, yellow, and black. Books can also be printed in black ink only or with one or more "spot" colors (a color of ink other than C, M, Y, or K).

ART COUNT How many images are in your project, and roughly how large are they (full page, quarter page, etc.)?

PAPER STOCK Your printer may have an inexpensive house sheet on hand, or perhaps there's a particular paper you want to work with.

COVER Case bound? Paperback? Saddle stitched?

BINDING Some binding techniques may take place at a bindery, a plant separate from the printer. This can add several days to the production schedule.

SPECIAL PROCESSES Extras can include special inks (metallic), varnishes, foil stamping, and die cuts.

Offset and Digital Printing

Most commercial printing is done either via offset lithography (using ink and plates) or via toner-based digital printing. These techniques are commonly used for any project bigger than a few hundred copies. When working with a commercial printer, the designer or publisher needs to prepare files carefully and communicate clearly to avoid mistakes in manufacturing. Most printing snafus get tracked back to designers who have provided faulty or incomplete files and ambiguous instructions.

SELECTING INK

An important choice to make early on is how many colors your book will need to be printed. Novels or nonfiction works usually require only black, while any book with full-color imagery will need at least four. Cyan, magenta, yellow, and black (known as process colors or CMYK) are used to create full-color imagery, but those aren't the only colors available for you to use.

Special colors called "spot colors" provide numerous rich and otherwise unobtainable tones and effects. They are typically chosen from the Pantone Matching System (PMS), a color specification system. Pantone swatch books are used to select specific colors, which are then identified by a special code. There are several books in the PMS library (uncoated, coated, metallic), so be sure to use the correct book when specifying colors in your file. All spot colors must be present in the design document as a specific color so that the document will separate into distinct printing plates, one for each ink. It is a good idea to attach a color chip to the hard copy of your document for the printer's reference.

Digital printing is usually four-color only; spot colors will be replaced by their CMYK equivalent.

SELECTING A PAPER STOCK

There are two categories of paper: coated, which has a smooth and sometimes glossy surface, and uncoated, which has a softer finish. To help in your selection, request swatch books to select the weight, surface, and color of paper that suits your vision. You can get swatch books from paper vendors or through the printer who in the end will secure the paper for you.

Once you have identified potential paper stocks and the binding method for your book, having a physical sample to hold will help you make well-informed final decisions. A paper dummy is a blank, bound sample put together from the specifications of your book (page count, size, text stock, and cover stock). Paper dummies expose physical problems that you may not think of otherwise. How does the paper stock feel? Is there enough contrast between the weight of the cover and interior? Once you open it, does the book stay open or flop shut?

FILE FORMATS

Images (such as photographs) should be saved as TIFF files for proper separation. Vector art (such as logos and line diagrams) should be saved as EPS files. JPEG, GIF, and PNG files are typically used for the web and are not suitable for print. Convert them to TIFF files.

IMAGES AND GRAPHICS

Any image or graphic placed in your document must be provided to the printer as a high-resolution file. Photos must be at least 300 dpi and line art should be between 900–1200 dpi. Keep in mind that applying a higher resolution to an image in Photoshop, or "rezzing it up," will only make the image blurry. Sometimes, low-resolution files are placed temporarily in a document to prevent huge files from bogging down your computer. On the marked-up hard copy of your document, mark where those photos occur by labeling them "FPO" (for position only). This indicates that the image must be replaced with a high-resolution file before it is sent to the printer.

Game Day: Submitting Your Final Files

Having spent days, weeks, or even years preparing files from your cozy desktop, now it's time to send your book to the printer. Take your time! It's easy to make big mistakes during this crucial phase.

1. DESIGNER RELEASES FILES TO PRINTER

Most page layout programs have a function that pulls together the elements needed to run your job, including the design file, artwork, and fonts. If your printer prefers to work with a high-res PDF, be sure to prepare it to their specifications (with bleed and crop marks, for example).

Always include a marked-up hard copy of the project for others to reference. Mark any spot colors, images that need special attention, and any other elements that you feel need explanation. Write clearly and directly on the mark-up (not on Post-it notes that can be removed or lost).

2. PRINTER PREPS FILES

Once the printer has the files, he or she will prepare them for their presses, check for potential problems, and set up the document into printer spreads. (These will be in the correct order and orientation when printed sheets are folded, cut, and bound.)

3. PROOFING DOCUMENTS

The printer will supply you with proofs to check before the job goes to press. Depending on the situation, you should receive two proofing documents. A color proof is generated to simulate as closely as possible how colors will appear on press. A blueline or content proof is for checking text, crossovers, and page sequencing.

Check carefully: Do all the images look clean and crisp? Has text reflowed or shifted? Have fonts loaded correctly? Again, write clearly and directly on both proofs.

Return the proofs to the printer in a timely manner and indicate how you wish to approve changes. You may only need a PDF to confirm minor edits. More significant changes should be made by the designer with new page layout files. A new round of proofs may also be in order (and will most likely cost you more money).

4. PRESS CHECK

Depending on the situation and your availability, plan on attending a press check at the printing plant. After the press has been adjusted for color and any kinks have been worked out, you will be asked to approve a printed sheet. Some minor adjustments to color can be made on press.

Practice Good File Hygiene

KEEP YOUR FOLDERS TIDY

Avoid having documents with names like "final_final_for_print." Maintain a folder that is exclusively for the most recent layout document. Archive older versions for reference. Label these older documents as versions (V1, V2 for example) to avoid confusion. Create a folder for links (which include all illustrations) and a folder for resources (important files that don't appear in the layout document but are pertinent to the book).

300 DPI, CMYK FOR ALL IMAGES

Print resolution should be 300 dpi at 100% for all images. Be sure all color files have been converted to CMYK.

DELETE ANY UNUSED SPOT COLORS

Make sure any spot color that may have found its way into your document and is no longer being used is deleted to avoid confusion.

DOUBLE-CHECK YOUR PAGE COUNT

Make sure you are working with multiples of sixteen for most signature books or multiples of two for books that bind single pages (like perfect, spiral, or side-stitched).

PROOFREAD AND CHECK SPELLING

Double and triple check your document for typos and grammatical errors. Be sure to run the page layout program's spell check function.

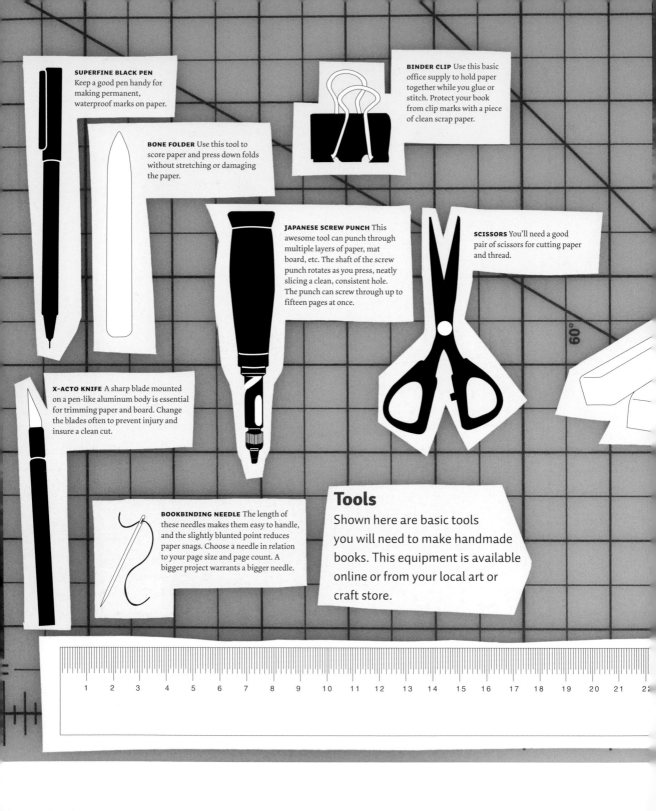

SUPERFINE BLACK PEN
Keep a good pen handy for making permanent, waterproof marks on paper.

BINDER CLIP Use this basic office supply to hold paper together while you glue or stitch. Protect your book from clip marks with a piece of clean scrap paper.

BONE FOLDER Use this tool to score paper and press down folds without stretching or damaging the paper.

JAPANESE SCREW PUNCH This awesome tool can punch through multiple layers of paper, mat board, etc. The shaft of the screw punch rotates as you press, neatly slicing a clean, consistent hole. The punch can screw through up to fifteen pages at once.

SCISSORS You'll need a good pair of scissors for cutting paper and thread.

X-ACTO KNIFE A sharp blade mounted on a pen-like aluminum body is essential for trimming paper and board. Change the blades often to prevent injury and insure a clean cut.

BOOKBINDING NEEDLE The length of these needles makes them easy to handle, and the slightly blunted point reduces paper snags. Choose a needle in relation to your page size and page count. A bigger project warrants a bigger needle.

Tools

Shown here are basic tools you will need to make handmade books. This equipment is available online or from your local art or craft store.

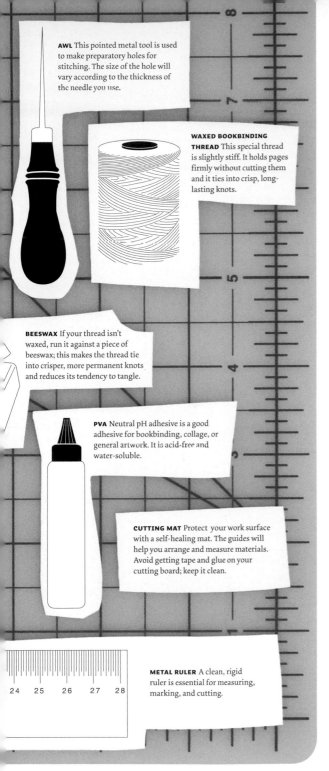

AWL This pointed metal tool is used to make preparatory holes for stitching. The size of the hole will vary according to the thickness of the needle you use.

WAXED BOOKBINDING THREAD This special thread is slightly stiff. It holds pages firmly without cutting them and it ties into crisp, long-lasting knots.

BEESWAX If your thread isn't waxed, run it against a piece of beeswax; this makes the thread tie into crisper, more permanent knots and reduces its tendency to tangle.

PVA Neutral pH adhesive is a good adhesive for bookbinding, collage, or general artwork. It is acid-free and water-soluble.

CUTTING MAT Protect your work surface with a self-healing mat. The guides will help you arrange and measure materials. Avoid getting tape and glue on your cutting board; keep it clean.

METAL RULER A clean, rigid ruler is essential for measuring, marking, and cutting.

HANDMADE BOOKS

By Viviana Cordova, Danielle Davis, and HyunSoo Lim

HANDMADE BOOKS ARE GREAT FOR SMALL EDITIONS DESIGNED FOR LIMITED DISTRIBUTION. A handcrafted book makes a terrific portfolio for an artist or designer, showing off production skills while creating an elegant showcase for the work inside. Artists' books and short-run editions of poetry can be beautifully and efficiently made by hand. Writers often collaborate with printers, designers, and book artists to make elegant literary editions.

Use the techniques described on the following pages to express your artistic side while controlling every aspect of the project, from the binding method to the choice of paper, thread, and more.

Start simple and work up to more difficult projects. Folded books require no stitching or gluing; these simple books can be made relatively quickly. Stitched books require needle and thread but allow for more versatility in size and page count. Add some glue to create complex books with intriguing covers and lush endpapers.

20–25 MINUTES

DIFFICULTY LEVEL

TOOLS

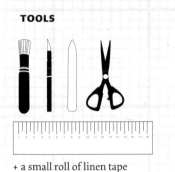

+ a small roll of linen tape

SELECTING PAPER
Choose a mid-weight paper for this project. If the paper is too heavy, it won't hold the fold well.

NO GLUE
This method requires no glue! Small pieces of linen tape are used to attach the pages to the cover.

FRENCH FOLD
The sheet is folded so that the folded edge is along the outside edge of the book, not the inside.

Circle Accordion Book

A circle accordion makes a terrific notebook, exhibition catalog, or photo album. This technique is easy to try because of its simple folding and construction methods.

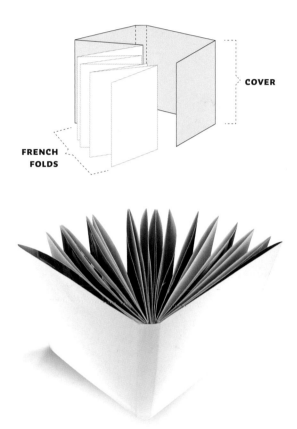

COVER

FRENCH FOLDS

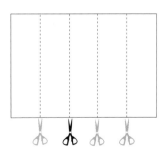

1. CUTTING THE PAPER
Cut a large sheet of paper into five equal strips. In this example the strips are 6 × 22 inches. Pick one strip of paper to be the cover. Cut off 1/2 inch to make the cover strip 6 × 21 1/2 inches.

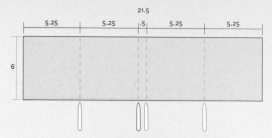

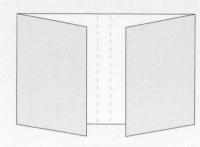

2. SCORING THE COVER
Measure, mark, and score two sets of two lines that are 5.25 inches apart (four lines total), starting from the two outer edges of the cover. (Score on the back side of the paper). You should have a 1/2-inch spine in the center.

3. FORMING THE COVER
Fold each edge in to the closest center fold.

4. FORMING THE PAGES
With the remaining strips, trim 1 inch off the long dimension to create four strips that are 6 × 21 inches each.

5. FOLDING THE PAGES
Score down the center of each strip. Fold, then crease well with a bone folder.

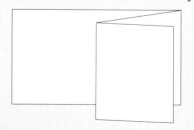

6. FOLDING AGAIN
Keeping the paper folded, bring one end back to the folded edge, creasing that end in half, to create a French fold. Each folded sheet will now be 6 × 5.25 inches.

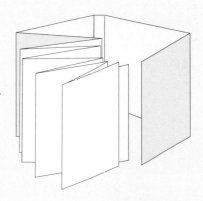

7. MORE FOLDED PAGES

Turn the paper over and bring the other end to the folded edge, again creating a French fold. Fold additional pages in the same manner.

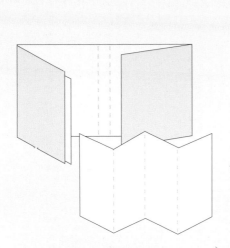

8. CREATING A SPINE

Cut two pieces of linen tape (shown in blue) slightly shorter than the height of your book Remove the backing from one piece of tape and center it so that half of it attaches to the edge of the cover and half remains available and sticky. Attach the French-folded sheet by aligning it with the cover and pressing down on the available half of the tape.

9. FINISHING THE ACCORDION

Continue to tape and attach pages until you get to the last one. Tape the last page to the back edge of the cover in the same manner as you attached the first page.

SEVEN VICES

This book was made to document an art installation. Making the book allowed the artist to create a permanent record of this temporary exhibition. Designed by Viviana Cordova.

BRAIN *DUMP*

doodle adventures in general education

15–20 MINUTES

DIFFICULTY LEVEL

Single Signature Pamphlet

The pamphlet stitch is the simplest and most versatile bookbinding technique. The pamphlet stitch utilizes three holes to attach the signature to the cover. For larger pamphlets, five holes can be used for greater stability.

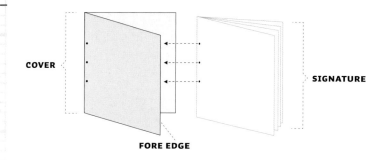

COVER

SIGNATURE

FORE EDGE

TOOLS

CHOOSING PAPER

Choose a mid-weight paper for the pages and a heavier cardstock for the cover.

FORE EDGE

The outer edges of the cover that are handled the most. Sturdier fore edges help protect the pages inside.

SIGNATURE

Two to eight folded sheets nested together to create the interior pages of a book.

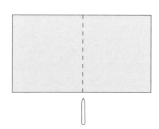

MAKING THE COVER

Cut a sheet of cover stock the appropriate size and score it down the middle. The cover can be 1/8 inch larger than the book's pages, or it can be flush. Gently fold to form the cover.

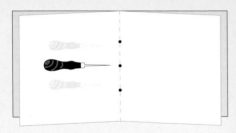

1. PUNCHING HOLES

Fold the inside pages and place them inside the cover. Punch a hole through the center of the spine, going through all the pages at once. Using an awl, punch two more holes equal distances from the center hole (making three holes in total).

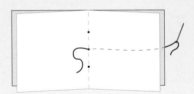

2. BEGINNING TO SEW

Cut a piece of thread three times the height of the book. Thread a needle, and begin by sewing from the inside of the pages and cover to the outside, starting from the center hole. Leave a tail of string long enough to tie together in the final steps.

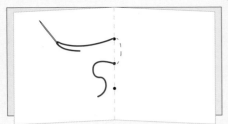

3. CENTER TO TOP

From the center hole, pass the needle through the top hole from the outside, pulling the thread through the cover and pages. The needle will come out inside the signature.

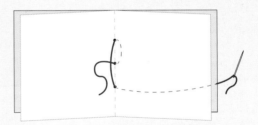

4. TOP TO BOTTOM

From the top hole, pass the needle out through the bottom hole from inside the signature to the outside of the cover, skipping the center hole.

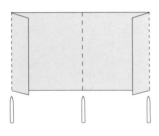

COVER STRENGTH

You can add extra strength to the fore edge of your cover by incorporating a narrow fold-in along the two vertical outer edges. Cut your cover 1 inch larger in width to accommodate the fold-ins. After scoring to create a fold line the same amount of inches from the left and right edges of the cover, gently fold along the line. Glue down the fold-ins if desired.

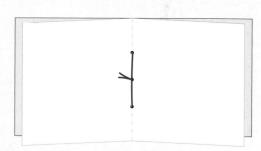

5. BOTTOM TO CENTER

From the bottom hole, pass the needle back through the center hole from the outside to the inside of the signature, making sure not to get your needle and thread caught in the thread that is already there.

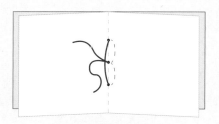

6. PULL TO TIGHTEN

After passing through the center hole, detach the needle and gently pull on the two loose thread ends to tighten. Tie the ends into a knot around the long stitch that is already there.

7. TRIM

Trim the excess thread, leaving enough to retie the book if necessary. To have the ending knot appear on the spine of the cover, start sewing from outside the cover instead of from inside the signature.

BRAIN DUMP This book consists entirely of doodles created during undergraduate lecture classes. Each image is categorized according to the general ed course in which it was jotted down. Designed by Danielle Davis.

VECTOR

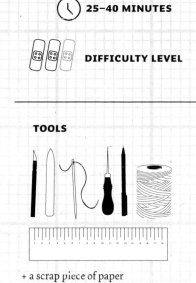

25–40 MINUTES

DIFFICULTY LEVEL

TOOLS

+ a scrap piece of paper

Multiple Signature Pamphlet

For books with multiple signatures, each signature section is sewn directly to the spine of the cover. The more signature sections, the wider the spine needs to be in order for the book to lie flat.

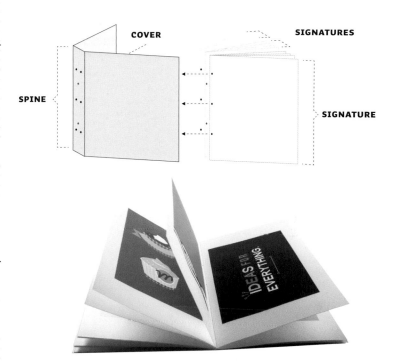

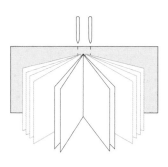

1. MAKING THE COVER

To create the cover, stack your folded signatures on top of each other and measure their thickness. This measurement will determine the width of the spine. This project has three sets of four folded sheets each for a total of twelve folded sheets (thirty-six pages). Transfer the spine measurement to your cover sheet by lightly marking the top and bottom of the sheet; score down the marked lines on the paper to create fold lines.

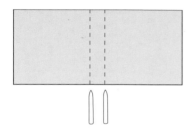

MAKING THE COVER (continued)
Fold along the scored lines to create the spine. Measure the height and width of the folded interior sheets and add an extra 1/8 inch to each; this will be the dimension of the front and back cover. Carefully cut the cover paper to size.

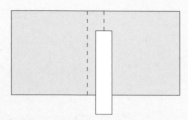

2. MAKING A SPINE TEMPLATE
Creating a template helps work out the hole positions that will be punched on the spine. Once planned out on the template, those measurements can be transferred to the actual spine. To make a template, cut a piece of scrap paper that is the exact size of the finished spine.

3. MARKING THE TEMPLATE
Mark three horizontal lines across the template where you want the holes to appear on the spine. Avoid making too many holes close together as this weakens the spine and could create tear points.

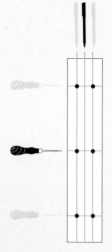

4. PUNCH THE HOLES
Because there are three signatures in this project, divide the width of the template into fourths. Mark vertical lines at each fourth along the template. The points where the first and third vertical lines and the horizontal lines cross are where the holes will be punched.

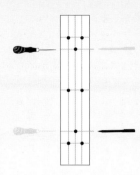

5. COMPLETING THE TEMPLATE

The outer signatures will be sewn with the traditional three-hole pamphlet stitch. The inner pages will be sewn with only two holes; mark these points near the top and bottom of the center line.

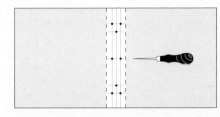

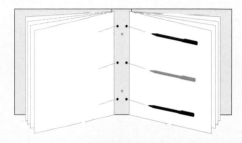

6. TEMPLATE TO COVER

Position the spine template over the outside of the cover and, using a needle or awl, punch the marked holes through the template and spine.

7. LINING UP THE SIGNATURES

Flip the cover so the inside faces up and line up each signature with the corresponding spine holes. Mark the holes from the spine onto the fold line of each signature and punch the holes.

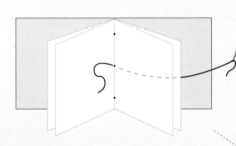

8. SEWING THE FIRST SIGNATURE

Nest the signature inside the cover and align the holes. Thread a needle and begin by sewing from the inside of the pages and cover to the outside, starting from the center hole. Leave a tail of thread long enough to tie together in the final steps.

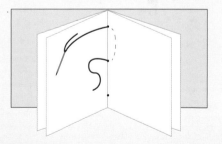

9. CENTER TO TOP

From the center hole, pass the needle through the top hole from the outside, pulling the thread through the cover and pages. The needle will come out inside the signature.

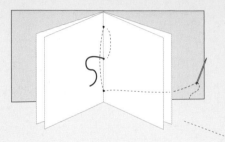

10. TOP TO BOTTOM

From the top hole, pass the needle out through the bottom hole from inside the signature to the outside of the cover, skipping the center hole.

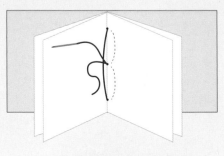

11. BOTTOM TO CENTER

From the bottom hole, pass the needle back through the center hole from the outside to the inside of the signature, making sure not to get your needle and thread caught in the thread that is already there.

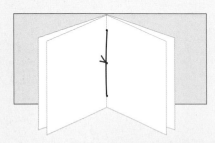

12. PULL TO TIGHTEN

After passing through the center hole, detach the needle and gently pull on the two loose thread ends to tighten. Tie the ends into a knot around the long center stitch, and trim the excess thread, leaving enough to retie if necessary.

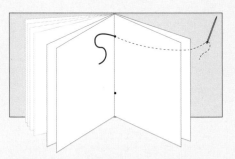

13. SECOND (MIDDLE) SIGNATURE

The second signature utilizes only two holes. Start by passing the threaded needle through the top hole, starting from inside the signature to the outside of the cover.

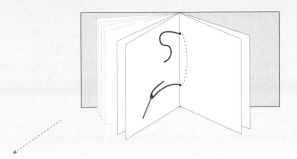

14. CENTER TO TOP

Travel down the spine and pass the needle through the bottom hole, from outside the cover to back inside the signature.

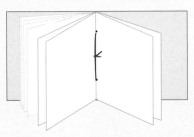

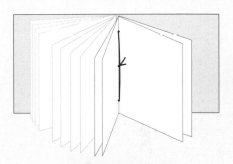

15. PULL TO TIGHTEN

After passing through the bottom hole, detach the needle and gently pull on the two loose thread ends to tighten. Tie the ends into a knot in the center and trim the excess thread.

16. THIRD SIGNATURE

The last signature is sewn the same as the first. Repeat steps 8–12 to finish assembling the book.

VECTOR

This book is a portfolio of vector illustrations. To make the book even more colorful and fun, the designer sewed it with red thread. Designed by Danielle Davis.

VARIED

DIFFICULTY LEVEL

TOOLS

CHOOSING PAPER

For a softcover book, the cover paper should be a little heavier than your pages and cut flush with the pages. A hard cover can be covered with fabric or decorative paper. Use flexible paper for the inside pages.

HINGED BOARD

A narrow strip of board works as a hinge for the final book cover, which opens and closes.

Stab Binding

Stab binding, also called Japanese stab binding, originally developed in Asia. It allows you to bind single sheets of paper with needle and thread. Sometimes stab binding is used with French folds, but single sheets are more common. This binding style works best with thin, flexible papers.

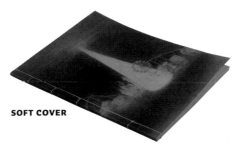

SOFT COVER

CHOOSING COVERS

With a stab binding, a soft cover is more functional than a hard cover, because the flexible surface opens more easily. A hard cover is more formal, however, and it will make the book last longer.

HARD COVER (NO SPINE)

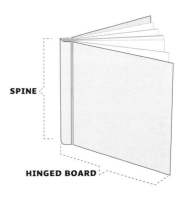

SPINE

HINGED BOARD

HARD COVER WITH SPINE

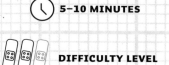

5–10 MINUTES

DIFFICULTY LEVEL

SOFT COVER

Softcover books are great for personal journals, sketchbooks, or anything that will be opened repeatedly.

1. CUTTING THE COVER

Measure and cut your cover papers and/or boards to the correct size, as shown here.

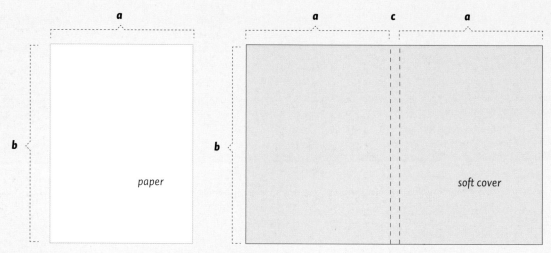

paper

soft cover

c = thickness of stack of papers

ENGLISH EXPRESSIONS

This book with a soft cover is a collection of English expressions assembled by a Korean student who carries it with her in her pocket or purse. Designed by HyunSoo Lim.

15–20 MINUTES

DIFFICULTY LEVEL

HARD COVER (NO SPINE)

Hardcover books are a great way to present your work in a professional manner that will showcase a high level of craftsmanship.

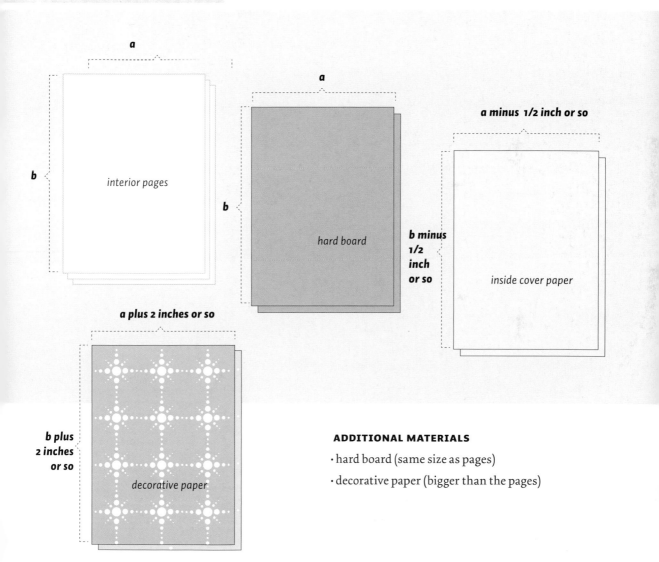

a

b

interior pages

a

b

hard board

a minus 1/2 inch or so

b minus 1/2 inch or so

inside cover paper

a plus 2 inches or so

b plus 2 inches or so

decorative paper

ADDITIONAL MATERIALS

· hard board (same size as pages)

· decorative paper (bigger than the pages)

1/4 1/8

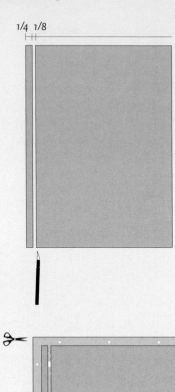

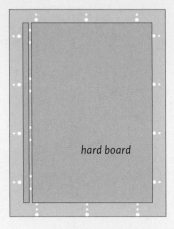

hard board

1. MAKING THE HINGE
Remove a 1/8-inch strip from the edge of the front cover board material, 1/4 or 1/2 inch from the edge.

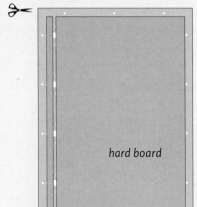

hard board

2. COVERING THE BOARD
With a brush, apply PVA glue across an entire sheet of decorative paper. Keeping the 1/8-inch gap, lay the two pieces of the front cover board in the middle of the glued paper.

3. SMOOTH THE PAPER
Cut the decorative paper so that 1/2 inch can overlap the side of the board. Smooth the decorative paper onto the cover board.

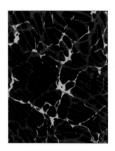

DECORATIVE PAPERS
You can use your own sketches, photographs, wrapping paper, or fabric as decorative paper.

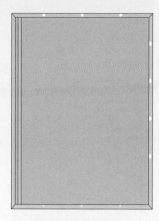

4. CREATING CORNERS

Cut off the corners of the decorative paper, about 1/8 inch from the board.

5. FOLD AND GLUE

Fold over the edges of the glued paper and makes sure the paper on the edges is smooth.

inside paper

6. INSIDE COVER PAPER

After the decorative paper has dried, glue the inside cover paper to hide the folded corners. This paper should be smaller than the hard cover but big enough to cover the tucks in the corners. Repeat steps 1–6 for back cover.

DIFFERENCE

This hardcover book uses a beautiful mix of materials. Designed by HyunSoo Lim. Photo by Dan Meyers.

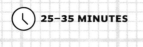

25–35 MINUTES

DIFFICULTY LEVEL

HARD COVER (WITH SPINE)

The spine of a hardcover book creates that true "book" feel. It gives the book stability and offers a high rate of longevity. Print your name or your book title on the spine for a more finished look when displayed on a shelf.

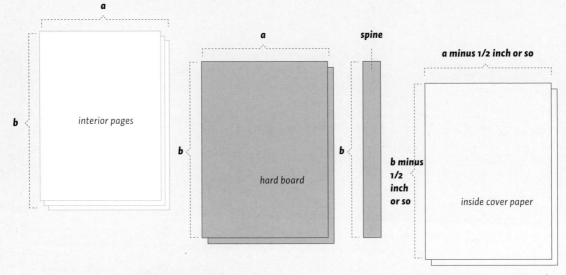

a

b

interior pages

a

b

hard board

spine

b

b minus 1/2 inch or so

a minus 1/2 inch or so

inside cover paper

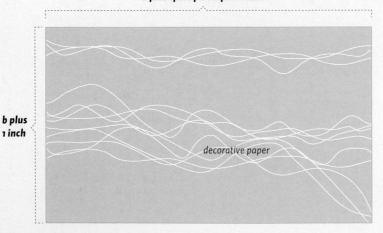

a plus spine plus a plus 1 inch

b plus 1 inch

decorative paper

ADDITIONAL MATERIALS

- hard board
  (same size as pages)
- inside cover paper
  (smaller than pages)
- decorative paper
  (width of page × 2) +
  (width of spine + 1 inch) ×
  (height of paper + 1 inch)

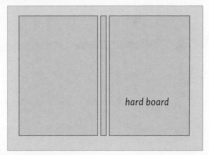

1. CUTTING THE BOARDS

For the covers, cut two boards that are the same height as your pages and 1/8 inch narrower than their width. For the spine, cut a board that is the height of the interior pages and the width of the thickness of the pages.

hard board

2. GLUING THE BOARDS

Glue the spine board in the middle of the decorative paper. Leave a gap between it and the two cover boards that is the width of two boards.

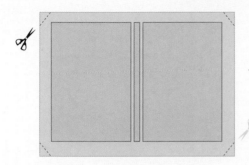

3. CREATING CORNERS

Cut off the corners of the decorative paper, about 1/8 inch from the board.

4. FOLDING THE EDGES

Smooth the glued paper into the grooves and around the cover boards, then fold it over the edges of the boards.

WAXED PAPER

Place a sheet of waxed paper between each glued piece when drying so they don't stick together.

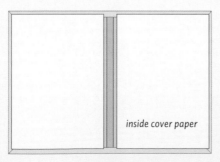

inside cover paper

5. INSIDE COVER PAPER

After the paper dries, add the inside cover paper. This paper should not cover the spine, as it will be hidden inside the stab binding. Put paper or sheets of board inside the cover to maintain the height of the spine; weight it with a few books until dry.

15–20 MINUTES

 DIFFICULTY LEVEL

BINDING THE PAGES

Stab binding uses stitches to connect the pages to each other and to the cover. In this technique, the construction is a visible part of the design. The stitches are both functional and decorative.

1. ASSEMBLING THE BOOK
Gather together your inside pages and your cover elements (soft or hard cover, with or without spine).

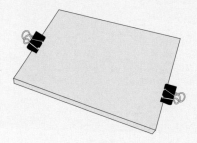

2. USING BINDER CLIPS
Double check that the paper and the cover are square. Slip them into binder clips. Use an extra sheet of board to protect the covers from clip marks.

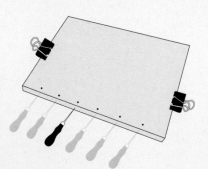

3. DRILLING THE HOLES
Drill the holes with a screw punch. The holes should be evenly spaced and follow the line of the spine. (Mark the holes before you drill.)

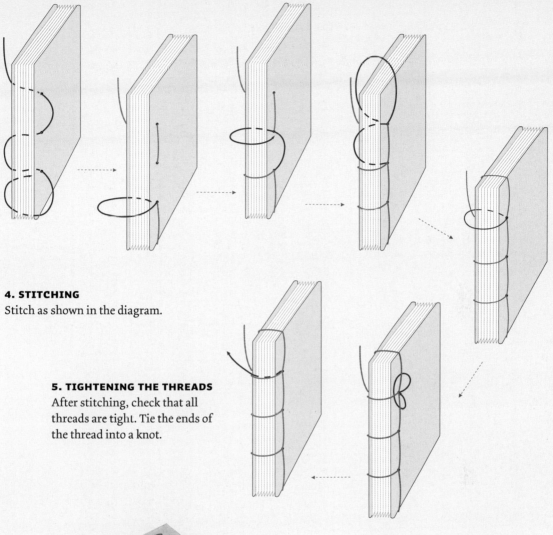

4. STITCHING

Stitch as shown in the diagram.

5. TIGHTENING THE THREADS

After stitching, check that all threads are tight. Tie the ends of the thread into a knot.

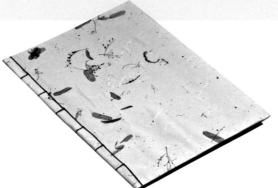

DATA BOOK

This book is used for gathering tickets, metro cards, napkins, and Polaroid prints taken while traveling. Designed by HyunSoo Lim. Photo by Dan Meyers.

INDIE INSPIRATION

Designer as Publisher—Artists' Books as Indie Publishing

DESIGNER AS PUBLISHER

by Kristian Bjørnard and Lindsey M. Muir

Traditionally, graphic designers have worked for clients, helping other people put ideas into print. Today, many designers are initiating their own projects, wielding their visual skills and knowledge of the publishing industry to become their own producers. These designers are at the forefront of the indie publishing movement. They are actively rejecting the established role of the graphic designer, who is called in to format an author's work after an editor and publisher have decided to produce it. Although designers give books their unique visual signature (especially in the case of complex visual works), they are often overlooked in press reviews and even author's acknowledgments, and they rarely share in a book's profits.

Why do designers become publishers? Some of these indie producers are seasoned book designers who, after years of working for clients, are eager to use their inside connections and hands-on experience to launch projects on their own. Others, starting with a single publication, use their abilities to realize a pet project or cherished idea, while still others strive to bring to light special content that is being overlooked by the mainstream publishing industry. Some designers are authors of the books they publish, while others work with writers and artists to generate content.

The desire to showcase text and image in the best way possible lies at the root of each project illustrated on the following pages. The designer as publisher is in a unique position to unify text, imagery, layout, and final production into a whole that is greater than its parts.

MCSWEENEY'S

Dave Eggers launched his literary zine *Timothy McSweeney's Quarterly Concern* in 1998. The journal was an immediate hit, recognized for its cheeky content and its playful design and typography. It is produced in multiple styles and formats, from bound books with elaborately decorated covers to a loose stack of chapbooks boxed together with binding board. The McSweeney's enterprise soon expanded to include books and additional journals, including the *Believer*.

FUEL

Based in the United Kingdom, Fuel was founded in 1991 as a design agency. Initially, Fuel pursued publishing as a side project, creating a magazine as well as two monographs of the firm's own work. Fuel's publishing venture has since evolved into a separate enterprise, Fuel Publishing, which now accounts for half the firm's total business. Fuel produces high-quality books about design, art, and popular culture. It works collaboratively with authors and artists to create distinctive books such as *BibliOdyssey*, a collection of images trawled from the far reaches of the web, and *Russian Criminal Tattoo*, an encyclopedia of body art from the archives of Danzig Baldaev and Sergei Vasiliev.

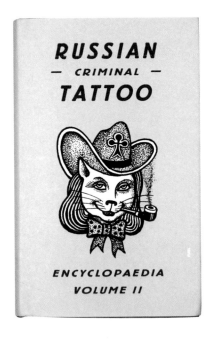

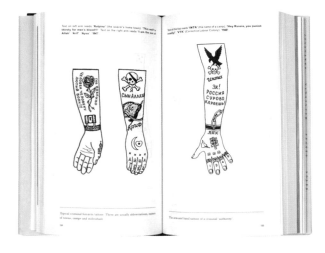

DRAWN & QUARTERLY

Drawn & Quarterly began in Canada in 1989, when Chris Oliveros decided to create an anthology magazine of the best North American comic artists. *Drawn & Quarterly Anthology* has become a full-color, 9-x-12-inch volume featuring work from an international slate of artists. In addition to producing two different comic artist anthologies (*Drawn & Quarterly* and *New Talent Anthology*), Drawn & Quarterly now publishes several comic book series and graphic novels, including Adrian Tomine's *Shortcomings* (below). What started with one man's love of comics has become a publishing house known for beautiful and thoughtful publications whose forms bend the line between comics and books. These publications have broadened the discourse on comic art worldwide.

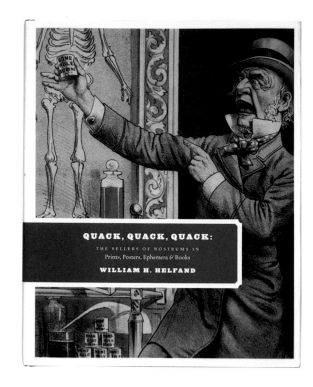

Jessica Helfand : Screen
: Essays on Graphic Design,
: New Media, and Visual Culture

: Criticism and commentary 1994–2001
: Twenty-three essays
: 200 pages
: Dedicated to Fiona + Malcolm
: Library of Congress Publication Data
: Helfand, Jessica
: Screen
: Introduction by John Maeda
: ISBN # 1-56898-320-4
: CONTENTS
: Myth of Real Time
: Electronic Typography
: Cult of the Scratchy
: Sensory Montage
: Age of the Behemoth
: The Death of Hierarchy
: The Big Reveal
: Essays on Silence, de Stijl, Spin,
: Narrative, and Paul Rand
: [etc.]
: 1. Visual communication.
: 1. Graphic arts.
: 1. Title.
: P93.5 .M45 2001
: 302.23-dc21
: 2001003629

WINTERHOUSE

Winterhouse, a partnership between William Drenttel and Jessica Helfand, functions as a design studio, consultancy, and publishing house. Winterhouse Editions publishes original works of fiction, poetry, design, and critical essays and republishes literature. Winterhouse also publishes the prestigious design blog Design Observer and the periodical *Under the Fold*.

Drenttel began working in this area with William Drenttel Editions, producing hand-printed and hand-bound limited editions of one hundred copies. Subsequent publications have increased in volume and are produced in various ways, sometimes in collaboration with larger publishing houses such as University of Chicago Press and Princeton Architectural Press. Winterhouse often focuses on material that has escaped the notice of other publishers. Some works are about design and visual culture, while others are pure text—*The National Security Strategy of the United States of America*, a document in the public domain, was published as a pocket-sized paperback after 9/11.

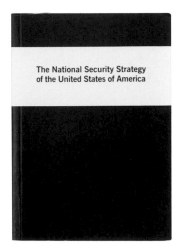

The National Security Strategy of the United States of America

GREYBULL

Based in Los Angeles, Greybull Press produces large-format, photography-based art books. Started by Roman Alonso and Lisa Eisner to publish Eisner's photographic work, Greybull has become an art-book publisher known for its unique content and exacting quality. The team (joined by Lorraine Wild) has remained autonomous from larger publishing companies in order to maintain control over all aspects of design and production. Many Greybull titles revolve around subcultures. *Hollywood Life* reveals the strange world of Hollywood homes; *Black Panthers 1968* looks at the visual culture of the black power movement; *Height of Fashion* takes a retrospective look at personal style.

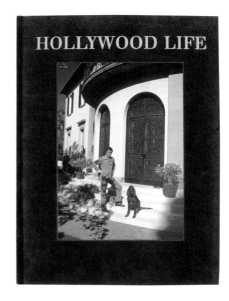

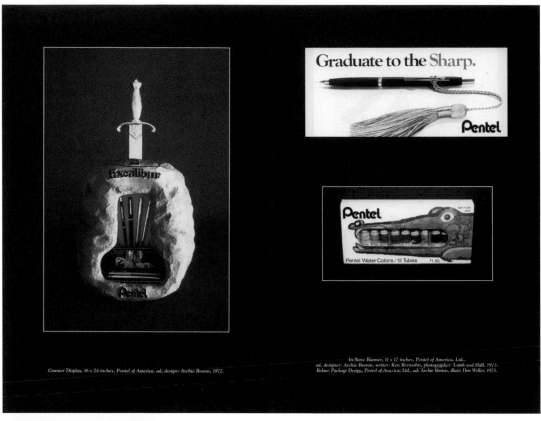

Counter Display, 16 x 24 inches, Pentel of America, ad, design: Archie Boston, 1972.

In-Store Banner, 11 x 17 inches, Pentel of America, Ltd.,
ad, designer: Archie Boston, writer: Ken Bernsohn, photographer: Lamb and Hall, 1973.
Below: Package Design, Pentel of America, Ltd., ad: Archie Boston, illust: Don Weller, 1973.

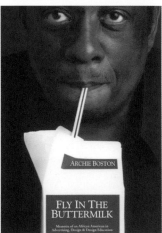

FLY IN THE BUTTERMILK

In 2001, designer and art director Archie Boston self-published *Fly in the Buttermilk* about the trials and tribulations of being a black male designer working within a white-dominated industry. Boston felt that his story needed to be heard, so he decided to voice it in print.

The first part of the book is a memoir of his life as a designer and educator within the field. The second half discusses Boston's personal views on design and the world of advertising. The book features much of Boston's award-winning work as a designer whose career spans thirty-five years.

This 186-page book is offset printed and bound into a sleek hardbound volume. Boston sells his book through his personal website and on Amazon. A part of the proceeds is donated to the Archie Boston Scholarship Fund at California State University, Long Beach.

HOW TO MAKE OUT IN THE SUPPLY ROOM

Los Angeles–based graphic designer Rachel Rifat self-published her book *How to Make Out in the Supply Room: Fun Things to Make and Do When the Boss Is Not Looking* during the fall of 2006. This clever book, which mimics the form of a writing pad, is a guide for creating crafts with materials from an office supply room. Rifat explains that if one gets caught reading her book while on the job, he or she can quickly flip the cover to disguise the book as a real writing pad. Her crafts range from paperclip necklaces to coffee Zen gardens to hole-punched frames. Each project is illustrated with color photos and step-by-step instructions. Rifat's thesis: it is better to be a creative employee than a disgruntled one. Rifat sold several copies of her hand-bound book to her friends, who convinced her to submit it to book agents. Within twenty-four hours of submission, the Sandra Dijkstra Literary Agency had agreed to represent the book, which will be published in 2009 by Running Press.

ARTISTS' BOOKS AS INDIE PUBLISHING

by Jennifer Tobias

THE INDIE PUBLICATION YOU HOLD IN YOUR HANDS IS AT ONCE NEW AND TRADITIONAL. On the one hand, today's independent publishing presents exciting new opportunities for artists, authors, and designers—everyone seeking a medium for their message. On the other hand, indie publishing has a tradition, from William Henry Fox Talbot's photographic album *The Pencil of Nature* (1844) to Dada manifestos of the 1920s to Ed Ruscha's landmark books of the 1960s. This latter body of work and the torrent of production it inspired are the focus of this essay. It will explore especially works that both embrace and critique dominant institutions—including the publishing industry.

The difference between book artists of yesterday and today is that contemporary artists are more willing to "work the system," using mainstream means for alternative ends. Many recent efforts operate as media-savvy nonprofits, engaging "the establishment" (commercial publishers, museums, galleries) in realizing a given idea. This phenomenon is not quite the same as going mainstream—call it slipstream instead. Like one cyclist drafting another, both move faster. Mainstream and indie publishing propel each other forward, creating a slingshot effect. Perhaps this compelling dynamic will encourage you, too, to literally take publishing into your own hands.

"Artist's book" is one of several contested terms describing artist-driven alternative publications.[1] Neither coffee table art books nor luxury *livres d'artiste*, these are books conceived as art or art that takes the form of a book. Only in retrospect has this work been recognized as a genre in its own right—a highly diverse one, ever reinventing itself.[2]

Postwar artists' books emerged from a confluence of vital art movements of the 1960s, including fluxus, letterism, situationism, pop, conceptualism, minimalism, and new attitudes to photography. In the period when happenings and installation art literally made the scene, artists were experimenting with mail art, page art, and concrete poetry. Meanwhile "little magazines" began to publish "paper architecture" and architect-driven criticism. Key to the emerging practice of book art—and to indies today—is the primacy of the artist-producer who mobilizes ubiquitous printing technologies for expressive ends.

Book artists exploit myriad production options for a wide range of purposes, be they purely formal, highly conceptual, documentary, poetic, or activist. Regardless of content, artists, authors, and publishers have in common a drive to communicate with others by any print means necessary. Of special relevance to indie publishers are artists who strive to mobilize mass media to reach a mass audience (though whether they do so remains a lively debate).

As examples here show, heady results can be coaxed from the now-antiquated mimeograph, the humble photocopy, and ordinary offset printing.[3] Often the "wow" of an artist's book is its brilliant union of form and idea, a sense that the idea "wants," in fact begs, to take the form it does. For example, consider the large-edition flipbook (a popular artists' books sub-genre).[4] To "flip" there must be a book, and it must have the precise paper stock, registration, binding, and trimming that offset printing provides so well. Book artists often make the reader aware of the unique characteristics of books, such as physical intimacy and tactility, sequence, pacing, typography, and text-to-image as well as image-to-image relationships. The book is no mere delivery mechanism, but a medium in its own right, intriguing for its conflation of art and codex into a genre that refuses to be either.

From the kitchen-table experiments of the 1960s to today's collaborations, the field of artists' books remains full of possibility. In an era of media consolidation and recent threats to free speech, one hopes that all types of indie publishing will thrive.

Ed Ruscha, *Twentysix Gasoline Stations,* 1963. © Ed Ruscha.
Courtesy Gagosian Gallery.

TWENTYSIX GASOLINE STATIONS THAT SHOOK THE WORLD[5]

Ed Ruscha (b. 1937) is key to the history of artists' books. In his truly formative works of the 1960s, in particular *Twentysix Gasoline Stations* (1963), Ruscha hit upon a smart, innovative form that brought together conceptualism, documentary photography, mass production, and the physicality of books—a true slipstreamer.[6]

Twentysix Gasoline Stations cleverly appropriated mainstream media forms for expressive ends. With characteristic understated wit, Ruscha used snapshot photography, ostensibly hands-off design, and low-end commercial printing to produce a high-concept, almost sublime work. The forty-eight-page offset book delivers just what it says: photos of gas stations in the Los Angeles area. Significantly, the book is undesigned by design, defaulting to printing conventions wherever possible. A photograph of each station is laid out simply and printed in dry, lo-fi black and white, minimally captioned in a nondescript font. Printed at a shop local to the artist, even the book's signature size is standard. The book is special not for its customization but for its banality.

Ruscha takes full advantage of the format of the book. The work's page-by-page progression evokes the exit-by-exit sequence of L.A. freeways, while a thumb-flip through it feels like speeding down the pike, themes also explored by Robert Venturi, Denise Scott Brown, and Steven Izenour in their book *Learning from Las Vegas* (1972).[7] Surprisingly, the diminutive photographs end up monumentalizing this usually invisible temple to American car culture.

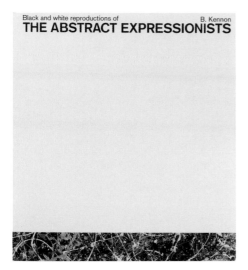

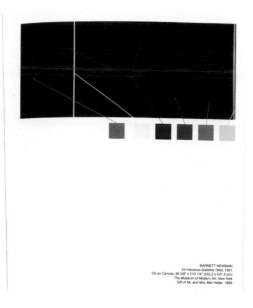

Brian Kennon, *Black and White Reproductions of the Abstract Expressionists*, 2002. Courtesy of the artist.

By taking the work from idea to printed book, Ruscha shared with many indie publishers (and drivers) the desire for autonomy. As he said after almost a decade of making books, "When I start on one of these books, I get to be impresario of the thing, I get to be majordomo, I get to be creator and total proprietor of the whole works, and I like that. It's nice. And I'm not biting my nails over whether the book is going to hit the charts or not."[8]

Decades later his work remains highly influential. A recent book that looks to and beyond it is Brian Kennon's *Black and White Reproductions of the Abstract Expressionists* (2002).[9] Here, too, what you see is what you see in fourteen offset pages. On each right-hand page is a black-and-white reproduction of a painting such as Barnett Newman's landmark *Vir Heroicus Sublimis* (1950–1951), keyed to color chips simulating—in four-color printing—the artist's hand-mixed paint.[10] The inclusion of Newman is particularly sly, for colors and their interrelationships are key to his work. Just as Walter Benjamin questioned the effects of reproduction on the "aura" of original artworks, in this deadpan book Kennon questions whether we "see" paintings as unique works to be encountered only live, or as mediated, logo-like symbols that take on lives of their own. The book references other works on this theme, such as Sherrie Levine's facsimiles of masterworks as they appear in standard art history textbooks.

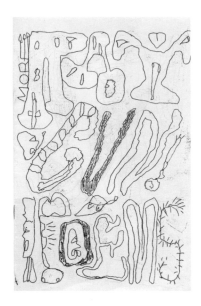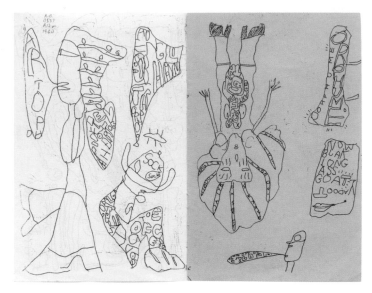

Claes Oldenburg, *More Ray Gun Poems*, 1960.

RAY GUNS AND TEMPORARY SERVICES

Three years before *Twentysix Gasoline Stations*, Claes Oldenburg (b. 1929) self-published *More Ray Gun Poems* (1960), a work that is significant today as part of a prototypical media package. This trippy, mimeographed, four-page word-image fusion was an ephemeral byproduct of Ray Gun Theater, a series of happenings at The Store, Oldenburg's SoHo alternative space. Ray Gun was part of a much larger movement to dematerialize art, and the printed page proved an excellent means for questioning traditional ideas about what art could be. This movement, which came to be known as conceptualism, rejected the unique object, the hand of the artist, noble subject matter, and precious materials, leaving only an idea—in this case the critique of art-making itself. (Ironically, even the most ephemeral

traces of these ideas are highly collectible today.) Oldenburg's *More Ray Gun Poems* was decidedly low tech. Says longtime artists' books advocate Martha Wilson, "The *Poems* were done on a stencil machine at Judson Memorial Church [a Greenwich Village alternative art space] on paper that was probably left over from Vietnam War protest marches or some such thing. The paper is crap. Then they were stenciled, which is crap, and then they were stapled together, which is more crap. If you look at the book in terms of materials it is a bunch of crap."[11]

Yet this crap carried, in its loopy lines, a provocative message about the nature of art, demonstrating that an idea, whether profound or perfunctory, may take any number of forms—even no physical form at all. In fact, *More Ray Gun Poems* involves a critique—but also an embrace—of the advertising and public relations industries thriving then (as now) on Madison Avenue. One wonders what the artist would have thought of today's press packages, event branding, and photo ops—themes he would engage later in works such as *Binoculars* (1991), a large-scale sculpture embedded in the facade of a major ad-agency building.[12]

Recent work by the contemporary trio Temporary Services (Brett Bloom, Marc Fischer, and Salem Collo-Julin) flows in a similar direction. Their "temporary services" include print as well as video projects, actions, a "mess hall," and a blog. Print productions range from free, downloadable PDFs to an offset book distributed by a mainstream publisher. *Prisoners' Inventions* (2003) packs a big punch into such a small, one-color trade book.[13] The work was a collaboration between Temporary Services and an incarcerated artist known only as Angelo, with whom a group member had been corresponding. "We arrived at the idea for the *Prisoners' Inventions* project through a series of casual discussions about inventions that Angelo sometimes mentioned in his letters. The idea of prisoners inventing wildly creative things to maintain greater personal autonomy and to bypass the restrictions that are imposed on them was immensely appealing to us."[14]

The book comprises Angelo's meticulous line drawings of innovations, such as an improvised, battery-operated tattoo needle. An entire section is devoted to cooking, including methods for heating water using an

Temporary Services, *Prisoners' Inventions*, 2003.

electrical outlet. For Angelo, as for many artist-producers, the creative process was one of discovery as he documented the inventions he had witnessed or created. Ironically, due to penal-system censorship, Angelo has never seen the published book.

Like *More Ray Gun Poems* before it, *Prisoners' Inventions* is a paper-based element in an unfolding series of activities. Just as *Poems* was a literal throwaway for Oldenburg's theater, an early version of *Inventions* was a casual pamphlet produced for a one-day event. And just as Oldenburg's experiments took on a life of their own, *Inventions* morphed into exhibitions and a website. As a result of these varied activities, media coverage further disseminated the idea—from slipstream to mainstream and back again.

Stinger Variation #1

This is a design that one of my cellies mass-produced. He could assemble one in about an hour using parts cannibalized from a couple of double-blade safety razors, a soft plastic lid from a tumbler, and some double insulated wire from an earphone plug.

I'm told that four- to six-blade stingers can be made, though I've never seen any and I'm dubious because of the insulation problems involved.

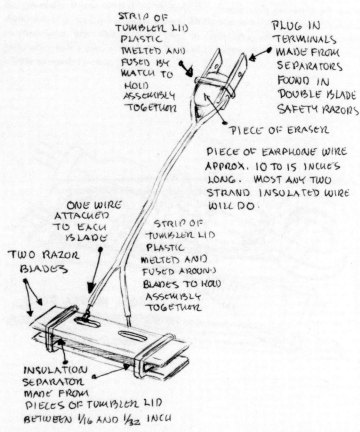

STRIP OF TUMBLER LID PLASTIC MELTED AND FUSED BY MATCH TO HOLD ASSEMBLY TOGETHER

PLUG IN TERMINALS MADE FROM SEPARATORS FOUND IN DOUBLE BLADE SAFETY RAZORS

PIECE OF ERASER

PIECE OF EARPHONE WIRE APPROX. 10 TO 15 INCHES LONG. MOST ANY TWO STRAND INSULATED WIRE WILL DO.

ONE WIRE ATTACHED TO EACH BLADE

STRIP OF TUMBLER LID PLASTIC MELTED AND FUSED AROUND BLADES TO HOLD ASSEMBLY TOGETHER

TWO RAZOR BLADES

INSULATION SEPARATOR MADE FROM PIECES OF TUMBLER LID BETWEEN 1/16 AND 1/32 INCH

Warning: Never plug the stinger in unless the blades are in the water, and never remove the stinger from the water while it's plugged in or it could blow up!

Temporary Services,
Prisoners' Inventions, 2003.

Stinger Variation #2

An interesting stinger design by one of my cellies. Simple and streamlined in appearance, but awkward to use, since without the play offered by a flexible wire, it is necessary to hand-hold the tumbler of water to be heated.

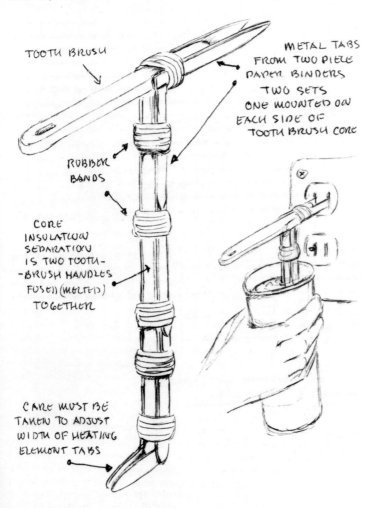

TOOTH BRUSH

METAL TABS FROM TWO PIECE PAPER BINDERS TWO SETS ONE MOUNTED ON EACH SIDE OF TOOTH BRUSH CORE

RUBBER BANDS

CORE INSULATION SEPARATION IS TWO TOOTH-BRUSH HANDLES FUSED (MELTED) TOGETHER

CARE MUST BE TAKEN TO ADJUST WIDTH OF HEATING ELEMENT TABS

Caution: Unplug the unit before removing it from the water.

Dieter Roth, *Daily Mirror*, 1970 reproduction of 1961 original.

HAZE AND MIRRORS

As we have seen, consciousness of media power is integral to the artist's book movement. Two examples—one well-known early work and a recent, under-recognized one—repurpose mainstream publications for slipstream ends. In the first version of his work *Daily Mirror* (1961), Dieter Roth (1930–1998, one of the fathers of artists' books) assembled pages from that newspaper then had them perfect bound and trimmed to two centimeters square.[15] The result is a tiny explosion of type and color, conflating journalism and advertising. Amazingly, this sugar cube of a book manages to evoke a vast media space like Times Square, producing the sense of information overload encountered there daily.

Honeymoon Suites (2003) by Penelope Umbrico appears to be a set of picture postcards glued along one edge, as found in souvenir stores. The pictures look like poorly printed horizons, with visible Benday dots of saturated red, orange, and purple. Oddly, no locations are identifiable—this could be Acapulco or Siberia. The images, the artist explains, are "taken directly from honeymoon resort brochures depicting happy, just-married couples in their honeymoon suites. I use only the ubiquitous candy-colored horizon, as seen through the windows in these idealized places."[16]

These cloying but striking images make us question what we see—or want to see—in advertising. The artist explains how formal choices, such as color printing and the

Penelope Umbrico, *Honeymoon Suites*, 2003. Courtesy of the artist.

postcard, push her theme: "The false color in the original source material reveals the constructed notion of romance through marketing. My horizons are a kind of global travel through the absurdity of the marketing of love."[17]

Here we fall in love with the idea of sunset in paradise, one we can buy and fly into. But is this sky so different from the one we see daily? Umbrico argues that even universal phenomena (sky, love) are literally mediated by advertising.

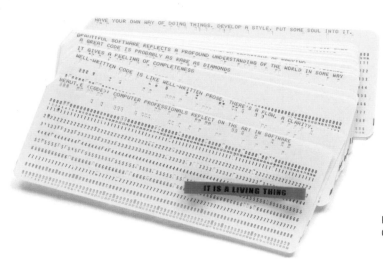

Karen Hamner, *Beaut.E(Code)*, 2002.
Courtesy of the artist.

BITSTREAMING

As digital media become ubiquitous, book artists seek to critically engage them. In Karen Hamner's *Beaut.E(Code)* (2002), the artist sought out one of the last U.S. computer punch-card printers to "output" programmer musings about the poetics of code.[18] Such statements as "It is a living thing" appear in dot matrix type at the top of each of thirty-four cards.

In a similar vein, David Byrne's *Envisioning Emotional Epistemological Information* (2003) pushes the notoriously limited vocabulary of Microsoft PowerPoint to expressive extremes.[19] The RGB-inspired color palette is maximized for eye-popping effect. Charting tools become power tools for the preposterous. Low-end typography is condensed, stretched, and skewed to its limits. Says Byrne, the work "is about taking subjective, even emotional, information and presenting it in a familiar audiovisual form using a medium in a way that is different, and possibly better, than what was intended....To use such a ridiculous piece of software, something so unyielding and proscribed for a supposed creative endeavor, is folly to begin with—and this absurdity is part of what allows me to connect emotionally with it."[20]

Though the creative process is low-tech in computer terms, its print production is on the high end, slip-cased and pricey compared to many artists' books. Yet a humble DVD version is included, with an original soundtrack by Byrne. With PowerPoint and a sound card in every PC, digital is the new mass media—one with a digital nature ready to be engaged. Just as Ruscha and Roth looked deep into the book, Hamner and Byrne help us to see the communications technology of our time through new, AV-enhanced eyes.

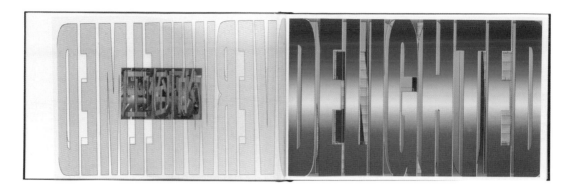

David Byrne, *Envisioning Emotional Epistemological Information*, 2003. Courtesy of the artist.

MULTIPLE FUTURES

Book artists today continue to use readily available production methods to investigate, critique, and communicate—with the twist that artists now are more likely to slipstream into the wider world of collectives, social media, and larger-scale publishing and distribution systems.

Digital production is now a common component of artists' books. Digital photography, typography, and layout are standard, and net-based advertising and distribution enable artists' books to reach a wider audience. Yet interest in traditional printing methods such as letterpress persist among contemporary book artists, reflecting and resisting the new ubiquity of digital media. According to Marshall Weber, director of collection development at artists' books publisher/distributor Booklyn, the six books his organization published this year have involved silkscreen, lithography, relief, and letterpress, as well as offset, photocopy, and short-run digital printing. Weber represents the general consensus in the artist's book community that new technologies such as print-on-demand are "just another tool and production method, so if an artist sees it as an appropriate tool they will use it."[21]

Because of increasing access to such technologies, alternative publishing is more democratic than ever. Then as now, its message can range from the conventional to the avant-garde—the same presses will churn out your baby pictures as easily as your radical manifesto. In this way book artists share common ground with today's indie publishers: accessible production methods, a climate conducive to open communication and debate, and the drive of people—like you—to join the data stream.

NOTES

1. Key works on the discipline, including its terminology, are Betty Bright, *No Longer Innocent: Book Art in America, 1960–1980* (New York: Granary, 2005); Johanna Drucker, *The Century of Artists' Books* (New York: Granary, 1995); Stefan Klima, *Artists Books: A Critical Survey of the Literature* (New York: Granary, 1998); Cornelia Lauf and Clive Phillpot, *Artist/Author: Contemporary Artists' Books* (New York: D.A.P., 1998); and Joan Lyons, ed., *Artists' Books: A Critical Anthology and Sourcebook* (Rochester: Visual Studies Workshop, 1985).

2. The Museum of Modern Art collection of artists' books is one of the largest in the world. For more on the collection see "Q: What is the Franklin Furness Artist Book Collection?," www.moma.org/research/library/library_faq.html#ff; accessed May 20, 2008.

3. For a brief history of mimeograph and photocopy publications, see R. Seth Friedman, *The Factsheet Five Zine Reader: The Best Writing from the Underground World of Zines* (New York: Three Rivers, 1997), 9–12.

4. Jörg Jochen Berns, *Daumenkino: The Flip Book Show* (Düsseldorf: Kunsthalle Düsseldorf, 2005).

5. Witty aphorism courtesy of Clive Phillpot, "Twenty-six Gasoline Stations that Shook the World: The Rise and Fall of Cheap Booklets as Art," *Art Libraries Journal* 18, no. 1 (1993).

6. The work is exceedingly well documented. The literature listed above in note 1 is a good place to start.

7. Robert Venturi, Denise Scott Brown, and Steven Izenour, *Learning from Las Vegas* (Cambridge: MIT Press, 1972).

8. Ed Ruscha, quoted in Bright, *No Longer Innocent*, 108.

9. Brian Kennon, *Black and White Reproductions of the Abstract Expressionists* (self-published, 2002).

10. For page scans see Second Cannons, publisher of artists' books, http://www.2ndcannons.com/BW-AbEx-detail-cover.html; accessed May 20, 2008.

11. Martha Wilson, quoted in Bright, *No Longer Innocent*, 116.

12. See the website of Claes Oldenburg and Coosje van Bruggen, http://www.oldenburgvanbruggen.com/binoculars.htm; accessed May 20, 2008.

13. Temporary Services, *Prisoners' Inventions* (Chicago: White Walls, 2005).

14. "Inmate Inventive Genius," quoted in Craig Buckley, "*Prisoners' Inventions*: An Interview with Temporary Services," on Static-ops.org, an online magazine; http://www.static-ops.org/essay_13.htm; accessed May 20, 2008. For Angelo's perspective, see "Inmate Inventive Genius," http://www.temporaryservices.org/Inmate_Inventive_Genius.html; accessed May 20, 2008.

15. Lauf and Phillpot, *Artist/Author*, 54. For more on Roth's books, see Dirk Dobke and Thomas Kellein, *Dieter Roth: Books and Multiples* (London: Hansjörg Mayer, 2004).

16. Penelope Umbrico, *Honeymoon Suites* (New York, 2003), n.p.

17. Ibid.

18. Karen Hamner, *Beaut.E(Code)* (self-published, 2002).

19. David Byrne, *Envisioning Emotional Epistemological Information*, slipcase (Gottingen: Steidl, 2003).

20. Ibid., slipcase. For a surprising history of PowerPoint, see Ian Parker, "Absolute PowerPoint," *New Yorker*, May 28, 2001, 76. For a design critique see the (independently published) Edward R. Tufte, *Beautiful Evidence* (Cheshire: Graphics Press, 2006).

21. Marshall Weber, personal communication, August 29, 2007. See also the website of Booklyn, an artists' books organization; http://www.booklyn.org; accessed May 20, 2008.

BIBLIOGRAPHY

PUBLISHING

Anderson, Chris. *The Long Tail: Why the Future of Business is Selling Less of More.* New York: Hyperion, 2006.

Greco, Albert N., Clara E. Rodriguez, and Robert M. Wharton. *The Culture and Commerce of Publishing in the 21st Century.* Palo Alto, CA: Stanford Business Books, 2007.

Kremer, John. *1001 Ways to Market Your Books.* Taos, NM: Open Horizons, 2006.

Poynter, Dan. *The Self-Publishing Manual: How to Write, Print, and Sell Your Own Book.* Santa Barbara, CA: Para, 2007.

Ross, Tom, and Marilyn Ross. *Complete Guide to Self Publishing: Everything You Need to Know to Write, Publish, Promote, and Sell Your Own Book.* New York: Writer's Digest Books, 2002.

University of Chicago Press. *The Chicago Manual of Style, 15th Edition.* Chicago: University of Chicago Press, 2003.

Weber, Steve. *Plug Your Book! Online Book Marketing for Authors, Book Publicity through Social Networking.* Falls Church, VA: Weber Books, 2007.

Zackheim, Sarah Parsons. *Getting Your Book Published for Dummies.* New York: Wiley, 2000.

DESIGN AND BOOK ARTS

Bartram, Alan. *Five Hundred Years of Book Design.* London: British Library, 2001.

Bringhurst, Robert. *The Elements of Typographic Style.* 1992. Reprint, Vancouver: Hartley and Marks, 1997.

Cockerell, Douglas. *Bookbinding: The Classic Arts and Crafts Manual.* Minneola, NY: Dover, 1996.

Eckersley, Richard, et al. *Glossary of Typesetting Terms.* Chicago: University of Chicago Press, 1994.

Felici, James. *The Complete Manual of Typography: A Guide to Setting Perfect Type.* Berkeley: Peachpit Press, 2003.

Hochuli, Jost, and Robin Kinross. *Designing Books: Practice and Theory.* London: Hyphen Press, 1996.

Kane, John. *A Type Primer.* London: Laurence King, 2002.

Lawson, Alexander. *Anatomy of a Typeface.* Boston: David R. Godine, 1990.

Lupton, Ellen. *Thinking with Type: A Guide for Designers, Writers, Editors, and Students.* New York: Princeton Architectural Press, 2004.

Müller-Brockmann, Josef. *Grid Systems in Graphic Design.* 1961. Reprint, Switzerland: Ram Publications, 1996.

Smith, Esther K. *How to Make Books: Fold, Cut & Stitch Your Way to a One-of-a-Kind Book.* New York: Potter Craft, 2007.

Spiekermann, Erik, and E. M. Ginger. *Stop Stealing Sheep and Find Out How Type Works.* Mountain View, CA: Adobe Press, 1993.

Williams, Robin. *The Non-Designer's Design Book: Design and Typographic Principles for the Visual Novice.* Berkeley: Peachpit Press, 1994.

INDEX